D1012259

WE'RE ON A MISSION FROM GOD

We're on a Mission from God

*The Generation X Guide to John Paul II,
the Catholic Church,
and the Real Meaning of Life*

by Mary Beth Bonacci

IGNATIUS PRESS   SAN FRANCISCO

© 1996 Ignatius Press, San Francisco
All rights reserved
ISBN 0-89870-567-3
Library of Congress catalogue number 95-78279
Printed in the United States of America ∞

Contents

EVANGELIZATION

RELATIONSHIPS

To Leo and Lavina, who gave me life and led me to Christ

Introduction

We love him—more than we love Mick Jagger, Cindy Crawford, or Michael Jordan. We travel thousands of miles, across continents and oceans, just to catch a glimpse of him in a stadium. We cheer wildly for him—screaming, crying, and chanting his name.

He is John Paul II, bishop of Rome, vicar of Christ, head of the worldwide Roman Catholic Church. We were with him at World Youth Day, whether in Manila, Denver, Czestochowa, Santiago de Compostela, or Buenos Aires. Some of us were physically present. Others of us were with him in spirit, wherever we were at the time.

Why do we love him so much? He doesn't sing our music, and he doesn't play pro sports. He's old enough to be our grandfather. He doesn't dress like a rock star, and he doesn't talk like a surfer.

And what's more, he tells us things that *everyone* knows we don't want to hear. He tells us to save sex for marriage. He tells us abortion is a great evil. He tells us contraception is contrary to our human dignity. He tells us to go to church and to pay attention while we're there. He tells us to listen to our parents. He reminds us to say our prayers.

Man, this guy knows *nothing* about appealing to youth.

Or maybe he does. Maybe he knows more than everyone else. Maybe he's figured out that what we're really looking for isn't sex, drugs, and rock and roll. Maybe he's found the deeper longing in our hearts— the one we're trying desperately to fill with all of that sex, drugs, and rock and roll; the one that seems to stay there no matter what we do.

We really aren't so different from anybody else. What we want is to be loved and to love—in a deep, abiding love that won't abandon us and won't degenerate into some kind of selfish, utilitarian use. That kind of love is hard to find in today's "get ahead at all costs" world.

John Paul II loves us. He radiates love. He brings that love everywhere he goes, and it's contagious. As soon as his plane lands for a World Youth Day event, picket signs disappear, protests dissolve, and skeptical anchorpersons suddenly gush admiring respect. It's as if he hauls nine hundred square miles of grace and love behind his plane, and it just settles on the city.

But there's more. The love he brings isn't just the love of a nice old man who happens to like kids. John Paul II brings supernatural love. He brings the love of Christ to us in a real, concrete, human way. When we respond to the love we see in John Paul II, we're really responding to the all-encompassing, all-embracing, all-forgiving love of God, the Author of Love.

We want love. He brings love. So what's so surprising?

The thing is, John Paul II does more than just love us. He teaches us. He has a lot to say to us—about our lives and about the emptiness we feel. He teaches us about the "narrow road" that God calls us to—the hard road that leads us out of our emptiness and into amazing happiness and fulfillment. He teaches us about the Christ who came that we might have life, and have it abundantly (Jn 10:10). He teaches us the way to that abundant life.

John Paul II brings us simple, profound truths. God loves us. Christ died for us. We find real love and real fulfillment through following Him. But he brings them to us in a new, powerful way—a way many of us have never seen before. So many of us haven't *really* learned about Christ. We may have been told to go to church and follow the rules. But we've never really been exposed to the powerful, personal, saving love of Christ or to the depth and beauty of His Catholic Church.

The problem is that sometimes it's hard to get past the big stadiums and the cheering throngs and the Polish accent and really *listen* to what John Paul II has to say to us. He says a lot in one speech. Often he says a lot in one *sentence*. There's real depth and insight in his words to us, but we sometimes miss it in all of the noise.

This book is about John Paul II and his message to us— to youth of all ages. It is about the life in Christ that liberates us. It is about the Church He founded. It is, most of all, about the insights into the mysteries of God that John Paul II brings to us in a single sentence or a single phrase. It's about the things he said to us but we missed because we couldn't go, or we went but he was too far away, or the sound system was lousy, or we were too tired because we'd been sleeping in a parking garage for the past week. This book is about the parts of the message that got lost in the excitement.

We love John Paul II because he doesn't "preach" to us. He makes the truth real, vibrant, and exciting. He wraps truth in an incredible love for us and brings it to us—an everlasting gift of fulfillment and life.

You can't find that in sex, drugs, *or* rock and roll.

I

Can Being a Christian
Make Me *Happy*?

The deepest source of our joy is the fact that the Father sent the Son to save the world.

— *John Paul II, Manila, 1995*

On this pilgrimage, our steps are guided by the words of Jesus Christ: "I came that they might have life, and have it abundantly."

— *John Paul II, Denver, 1993*

Do you ever feel really empty? Do you ever feel that there *must* be something more to life than what you've seen so far? Do you ever feel, no matter how much you have, that it's just never enough? Do you ever get that nagging, "I'm missing something" feeling?

If you're human, the answer is probably "yes". Sometimes, especially when things are bad, life can look like a real bummer. When you're facing family problems, or you've been rejected by someone important to you, or you're looking at the mess the world is in and wondering how it can ever survive, it's so easy to get discouraged.

Sometimes, even when things are going well, that

emptiness creeps up. We start to wonder if this is all there is. We crave more, but we can't define what it is we crave. We know we want more, but what?

For many people, life in America today is no picnic. Families are falling apart, pressures from society are crushing in at earlier and earlier ages, violent crime is on the rise, students bring guns to schools, and diseases from cancer and AIDS to alcoholism and bulimia run rampant. We've got a lot of really cool inventions, but we seem to be lacking real, honest love. The world can seem to be a very lonely, empty place.

It's easy, when things get bleak, to say, "Life is miserable enough. I can't be expected to live all of these religious rules, too." So we set out to try to make ourselves feel better—with sex, with booze, with drugs. Guess what? Life doesn't get any better. In fact, it tends to get worse.

Do you know why it doesn't get better? Because the discomfort we're feeling isn't there because we're not getting enough sex, or because our brains aren't messed up enough. Real unhappiness has a much deeper source. It comes, more often than not, from some kind of separation from God.

John Paul II knows that life can be difficult. He knows that you're suffering. And he goes through a whole lot of hassle to come to World Youth Day—for one reason. He has a message for you. That message is this: *Christ* is the way, the only way, to have that abundant life. He is the only way to real life. He is the only way to real joy.

Christ said, "I came that they might have life, and have it abundantly."

What does it mean to have life "abundantly"? It means, literally, to have a *lot* of life. It means to have a lot of good life—to have a really great, full, rich life. It means to have joy. If you put it that way, it's what everybody wants, right? We all want a really great life. We all want to experience joy.

But is that why *Christ* came? "I thought He came to lay down a bunch of rules and then die a horrible death because we're such idiots that we can't even recognize God when He's staring us in the face."

I don't think we often look at Christ, or at our faith in Him, as making our lives better. We see religion as a restriction on our lives—narrowing the field of what we can and can't do. We see it as making a sometimes miserable life even more miserable. We think, "Man, I could sure have a lot more fun if I weren't Catholic." We may follow the rules, because we see them as hoops to jump through so we can get into heaven. But we're not necessarily happy about it.

When John Paul II came to World Youth Day in Denver, he said something quite the opposite. He based many of his reflections on this passage. Christ came to give us abundant life—to make our lives *better*. He came to give us those big, full lives we've been looking for.

How can that be? Following God can be a bummer sometimes, can't it? You're expected to stand up for unpopular beliefs. You have to go to church when everyone else is sleeping in. You can't always do things you feel like doing.

What He gives in return, however, is far greater than any little sacrifice you may have to make. He made you for Himself. He made you to be happy only with Him. Regardless of the troubles you may encounter in this life, living in and through Him will provide a peace and a tranquillity that no other life, even life on "easy street", could ever give.

Christ didn't come just to lay down rules. He came because there was a huge rift between God and man—a rift that went clear back to Adam. We were messing up— we weren't loving. We were trying to find happiness apart from Him, and it wasn't working. It wasn't working because it couldn't work. He came to heal that rift, to open the door so that we could be united with God again and have that connection that leads to joy, to "abundant life."

Christ didn't come just to lay down rules. He came because there was a huge rift between God and man.

Christ gives abundant life in another way. Abundant means "a lot". Volume, quantity. What's the most life you could get? Life that goes on and on and on—everlasting life. That's what Christ offers us. Not only can we find happiness, but we can find *eternal* happiness: joy that never ends. In this life and the next, God is the way to go. He's the only key to real happiness.

That's what John Paul II's trips to World Youth Day are all about. That's also what this book is all about. World Youth Day is a pilgrimage. But so is life. And on that pilgrimage, our steps can be guided by a whole lot of different influences. Some people's steps are guided only by what feels good to them at the moment. Some are guided by what their friends say. Some are guided by a crystal or a guru in the desert.

None of those will lead to abundant life. If we really want joy, if we want that fullness of life that can never,

ever be taken away from us, Christ is the answer. He's the only answer. He is not only the way, but also the truth and the life.

Want it? Read on.

2

What's the Meaning of Life?

Life is a gift of a certain period of time in which each of us faces a challenge which life itself brings: the challenge of having a purpose, a destiny, and of striving for it. The opposite is to spend our lives on the surface of things, to "lose" our lives in futility; never to discover in ourselves the capacity for good and for real solidarity, and therefore never to discover the path to true happiness. Too many young people do not realize that they themselves are the ones who are mainly responsible for giving a worthwhile meaning to their lives.

— *John Paul II, Manila, 1995*

Since you have your life ahead of you, I invite you to decide definitely the direction of your way.

— *John Paul II, Santiago de Compostela, 1989*

Why am I here? Why am I alive at all? What must I do?

— *John Paul II, Denver, 1993*

Good questions. You've asked them. I've asked them. Nice to know that the Pope asks them, too.

Of course, I don't think that John Paul II was necessarily asking them about *himself* at this point. ("What is this place? Who are all of these kids?") I think he has a pretty good line on who he is, where he's going, and what he's supposed to do.

It's nice to know, however, that he's *aware* of the questions. It means he's asked them. He knows that *we* ask them. He understands how we feel when we ask them ("Oh, my gosh, my life is a mess. What am I doing? Why am I *here*?"). What's more, he defends our right to ask them. In fact, he says that "to fail to ask these basic questions is to miss the great adventure of the search for the truth about life."

Have you ever known people who failed to ask these questions or failed to take these questions *seriously*? You know, the kind who just take life as it comes, never really trying to understand or find deeper meaning, living from one fun time to the next. They're the ones who "lose their lives in futility". It doesn't seem like a bad way to live—during the fun times. But when the bad times hit, or when they're alone, or when the end begins to loom near, it can be a little scary. They don't need fun anymore. They need answers. And they've never bothered finding those answers.

In Manila, John Paul II said that we're the ones responsible for giving our lives meaning. What does that mean? Do we just decide, "Okay, my life's meaning is in collecting as many beer cans as is humanly possible. That search for aluminum will give my life fulfillment." Hardly. He said that missing our purpose means never discovering in ourselves the capacity for solidarity and for good. Where does that capacity come from? It comes from our relationship with Christ.

St. Augustine once said, "Our hearts were made for Thee, O Lord, and they will not rest until they rest in

Thee." When God created us, He built a little "God-shaped hole" into each of us. There is a vacuum, a space, a vacancy in the deepest recesses of our hearts. It's an emptiness that can be filled only by God. We need to love Him, to follow Him, and to do His will for our lives.

A lot of people profess to be Christians, try to follow the rules and avoid the big sins. But they feel that emptiness of the God-shaped hole, and they work like crazy at filling it up—with anything but God. They try to fill it with boyfriends or girlfriends, parties, beer, even work. Guess what? It doesn't work. Nothing else quite fits. Not only does it not work, but trying to shove anything else into that hole tends to ruin it. How many relationships have been destroyed because one or both expected too much from the other? They made the other person into God and expected the other to give their lives meaning, to fill that cosmic void in their lives. No one is God but God. And no one else fits in His space.

When the tenth year of partying or the tenth girlfriend doesn't get rid of the emptiness any more than the first, we may start to realize that there must be more somewhere.

We figure out why we're here only when we really give ourselves over to Him—when we decide we're going to do more than just follow the external rules. We need to decide really to love Him, as we'd love someone on earth. We need to decide that we're going to put Him first in our lives, we're going to let Him *into* our hearts, and we're going to turn our lives over to Him. We need to stop running away from Him and chasing after false gods, whatever they are. Those gods just lead to futility.

Finding the meaning of life involves more than just *knowing* with our brains that God is our only happiness. We need to *realize* it in our hearts and to allow Him to fill the God-shaped hole.

We may *know* that God is supposed to be the goal, but the search is in really *realizing* that and *wanting* Him above all else. Sometimes we don't realize it until we've been burned a couple of times. When the tenth year of partying or the tenth girlfriend doesn't get rid of the emptiness any more than the first, we may start to realize that there must be more somewhere. Maybe He put us here for something bigger. And maybe, if we follow Him and love Him above all else, He'll show us what that is.

I get the feeling that John Paul II has asked these questions. He's been on the search, and he's found the answer. Not just in his brain, but in the core of his being. He knows what he's supposed to do, and he's doing it with every drop of life in him. I mean, the guy works *hard*. He's under more stress than probably anyone in the world. He's responsible for the souls of a *billion* Catholics. But there's a peace, a radiance about him. Everyone at World Youth Day sees it. It's the radiance of holiness, the happiness that comes from knowing who he is, why he's here, and Who's in charge.

He is moving toward a goal. He has a purpose and a destiny, and he's striving for it.

You can have that, too. And if you do, you'll be happy: for a *long* time.

3

How Holy Do I Have to Be?

The One who has called you to Denver, and who can call you at any stage of your pilgrimage through life, wants you to have the treasure of knowing Him more fully. He wants to occupy the central place in your hearts, and therefore He purifies your love and tests your courage.

— *John Paul II, Denver, 1993*

What exactly does it take to be a "Christian"? How "into it" do you have to be?

A lot of people I've known say, "Yeah, sure I'm a Christian. I go to church on Sundays once in a while. And I think I'm basically a good person. I don't go all overboard or anything." Is that enough to be a follower of Christ? Is He happy when we just throw Him a little attention once in a while, when we're not too busy with what's *really* going on in our lives, like school and cars and the opposite sex? Does He just "take whatever He can get" from us?

John Paul II doesn't seem to think so. He says that Christ wants to occupy the "central place in our hearts". He wants to be *numero uno*, first and foremost, the main event in our lives. He wants the central place in our hearts.

He's not making this up out of thin air. He's taking it from what God told us. "Because thou art lukewarm, and neither hot nor cold, I will vomit thee out of my mouth" (Rev 3:15–16) Whoa! We thought He was grateful when we threw Him little crumbs of attention. We thought we were doing really well when we were "basically a good person". If all we're striving for is to be "basically a good person", and to put God into some neat little un-threatening corner in our hearts, we've got trouble. We're being lukewarm, and He doesn't like that. Not at all. When was the last time someone threatened to vomit you out of his mouth? It's not a pretty picture.

If all we're striving for is to be "basically a good person", and to put God into some neat little unthreatening corner in our hearts, we've got trouble.

So how does He want us to be? He wants us to be hot. He wants us on fire for Him. He wants us in love with Him. How do you act when you're in love? Do you do only what you absolutely have to in order to hang on to the relationship? Not if you really love. This person is constantly on your mind. You constantly want to please him. You want to be with him, to communicate, and you both want to get to know each other better. You don't say, "I spent *last* Sunday with you. Again now? How long do I have to stay? Is an hour enough?"

God wants us to be in love with Him. He wants us to be on fire for Him. He wants to be on our minds. He wants to be central in our hearts.

Why? Is this an ego thing for God? Does He just love to have people thinking about Him? What good could that possibly do Him? He's God—He doesn't need an ego. He already knows how great He is.

He wants us to think of Him because it's best for *us*. He made us with these big God-shaped holes in our hearts, and only filling them with God can possibly make us happy. Unfortunately, as we've seen, we're slow learners, and we keep trying to fill that hole with fun, or things, or whatever. It doesn't work, but we can be pretty stubborn.

So how does He bring us back once we've shoved Him into a corner? Simple. He "purifies your love and tests your courage". He reminds us how much we need Him. He lets us suffer a little. Or a lot.

Have you ever forgotten about God when things were going well? I have. It's easy. You don't really need Him around. You're doing just fine on your own. But then the wind shifts, and suddenly things aren't going so well. Life takes a turn for the worse, and there's not a dang thing you can do about it. You need somebody a lot bigger than you—to straighten things out, to give you strength, to see you through. God's suddenly back behind the wheel.

Nothing's really changed. God was at the wheel in the good times, too. He gave you the good times. You just forgot, and the God-shaped hole emptied out. And with that hole empty, you can't be happy for long. You're missing out on the real source. You're focused on the short term and risking the long term. And God loves you too much to leave you that way. So He gives you a little wake-up call. Pain. Suffering. Those desperate reminders that, in good times or bad, we need God. In the end, He's all we need.

How good a Christian are you? Is Christ in "the central

place in your heart"? Or do you have Him boxed up in a corner somewhere while you're "basically a good person"? Are you just lukewarm?

If that's the way it is, look out. He already told you what He'd do. And I don't think you'd like it.

4

Why the Catholic Church?

Our faith has historical foundations; it is not something vague and transient.

— *John Paul II, Santiago de Compostela, 1989*

We know that Christ never abandons His Church.

— *John Paul II, Denver, 1993*

When I was in high school, one of the most confusing things I had to deal with was figuring out what to believe. My parents believed one thing, my friends believed eighty million other things; my Church believed one thing, and their churches believed eighty million other things. Our teacher told us we had to "determine our own values systems" and decide for ourselves what we believed about everything. I felt a little young and ill equipped to be making determinations for myself on the morality of nuclear war or the doctrine of transubstantiation. I had to trust someone, but whom? Was I supposed to find experts for each separate issue? Do research? Examine conflicting opinions? Guess? Was I supposed to believe something just because the Catholic Church said I should?

When it comes to theological matters, most Protestant churches believe that the answers are in the Bible and that the Holy Spirit will help the individual reader understand what to believe. Unfortunately, as they all examine these things individually, they often come to conflicting conclusions about what is right. And then, often, their churches split, and new denominations are formed. There are thousands of them.

A lot of Catholics want to take a similar approach to their faith. They want to look at each issue for themselves and decide if they think that the Church is "right" on this issue. They then, while still calling themselves Catholic, want to practice only those tenets or beliefs they happen to agree with.

Isn't that a valid way to function as a Catholic? Don't we have a right to decide for ourselves what to believe?

We have to start with a more fundamental question. Why does the Church hold the teachings she holds? Is it because we pick a really smart guy to be pope, and then we have him study an issue very carefully, so when he decides something we're pretty sure he's right? Are we putting our faith in a guy and a system of teaching just because it's easier than figuring it out for ourselves?

No. The Church has never pretended that she teaches on her own authority. We believe that the Catholic Church teaches with the authority of Jesus Christ. Pretty big claim to make? Yes. Why would we make it? Because Christ Himself told us so—several times. He told Peter, the first pope, "Thou are Peter, and on this rock I will build my Church, and the gates of hell will not prevail against it. I will give you the keys to the kingdom of heaven; whatever you bind on earth will be bound in heaven" (Mt 16:18–19). And then again, before He ascended into heaven, He said, "All authority in heaven and on earth has been given to me. Go therefore and make disciples of all nations . . . and teach them to obey everything I have commanded you. And surely I am with you always, to the very end of time" (Mt 28:18–20).

Every single church that exists was started by *someone*. Lutherans know that their church was started by Martin Luther. Charles Taize Russell started the Jehovah's Witnesses. Steve Green founded the Vineyard Church.

Who first founded the Catholic Church? Jesus Christ. That's right. The Big Guy Himself, before He ascended into heaven, left us a Church, with a visible leader, the pope (see Mt 28:16; Mt 16:18-20). The Church isn't just a human reality. She's also a divine reality. She has ties not only in this world but in the world to come.

It makes sense. Christ came to give us the good news of salvation. That good news wasn't just for men of His time but for men of all time. So would He just leave the rest of us twisting in the wind—left with a hard-to-understand book and expected to figure things out for ourselves? No. Just as the Founding Fathers left us a Supreme Court to interpret the Constitution, so Christ left us with a living body to help us understand His will for us in all generations. That living body is the Catholic Church.

But, unlike the Supreme Court, the Church is not a cold, functional institution but, rather, a living reality—so real, in fact, that the Catholic Church even has a gender. The Church is female, "the bride of Christ". That's why we refer to the Church as "she". And Christ, like any spouse, loves His bride, gives Himself to her completely, and remains with her always.

So the Church has a lot of responsibility and a lot of power. Our rules bind not just on earth but in heaven, too.

Does this mean that the pope can decide tomorrow that beagles are sacred, or that it's a sin to part your hair in the middle, or that there are four persons in the Trinity? No. The Church's job is to protect and transmit Christ's teaching, not make up her own. But time goes on, and new questions arise about old doctrines. ("Is the pill a form of artificial birth control? Is it moral to conceive a baby in a test tube? What do we do about nuclear weapons?") We need the Holy Spirit's guidance to get the answers. That is what the Church does. We're not making things up for ourselves. Christ promised to stay with us.

Sure, we can decide for ourselves what to believe. Anything else would be absurd. Other people can't control our minds.

The Church's job is to protect and transmit Christ's teaching, not make up her own.

But to be *Catholic* means to choose to believe this— that Jesus Christ is God, that He died for our sins, and that He left an infallible Church that protects and transmits His teaching and His love to all generations. Either we believe that the Catholic Church teaches with the authority of Christ, or we don't. If we do, it would be absurd to pick and choose which Church teachings to believe. That would be deciding to disagree with Christ. If we don't believe that the Church teaches with the authority of Christ, why bother? We've rejected the defining tenet of Catholicism. We're not Catholic.

It's important that you, as a Catholic, know what your Church teaches. Fortunately for you, knowing those teachings is easier than ever. If you don't own a copy of the *Catechism of the Catholic Church*, get one. You can find it at any Catholic bookstore. In this book, all of the Church's primary teachings are collected in one volume. Don't listen to people who say, "The Catechism is just for bishops and teachers." It's for *all* Catholics and anyone else who is interested in the Church. It's for *you*. It's the final word on what the Church teaches—there's no better reference book in the world. You don't have to read it from cover to cover. (Although that's not a bad idea.) Keep it around to consult when you have questions. The answers are there.

Accepting the authority of the Catholic Church is not "unthinking", nor is it a cop-out. To believe something because the Catholic Church teaches it is to believe, with John Paul II, that "Christ never abandons His Church." I can't think of anyone's authority I would rather accept.

5

What's a Sacrament?

This immense mystery of love is made present to us through Holy Church's sacraments.

— *John Paul II, Denver, 1993*

Christ left us a Church. That's nice. We have a teaching body to help us understand right and wrong. That's helpful. But what else does the Church do for us now? Does she just provide us with a set of rules and a building so we won't be rained on while we pray?

The Catholic Church is not just a teacher or a convenient network of buildings. She is Christ's instrument of salvation—she is a vehicle through which He sends His love into the world. How does He do that? John Paul II, in the above quote, points out one of the most important ways—the sacraments.

Sacraments, for those of you who weren't paying attention during your CCD classes, are visible acts or signs, instituted by Christ to give us *grace*. Grace in this case isn't the ability to dance ballet without falling on our faces. Grace is God's action in our lives and in our hearts. It is the presence and activity of the Holy Spirit guiding our lives and our decisions. It is the spiritual fuel we need to follow God and overcome temptation. We can receive grace in a lot of ways—praying, doing good works, obeying the commandments. But we receive extra large doses of grace in the sacraments.

Christ instituted seven sacraments: baptism, confession, the Eucharist, confirmation, marriage, holy orders, and anointing of the sick. If you're Catholic, you've probably received several of these sacraments already, and you should be receiving two, namely, confession and the Eucharist, on a regular basis.

One of the primary traits of a sacrament is that it involves some kind of outward, physical sign. In baptism, water is poured on the head. In confirmation, we're anointed with oil. Each sacrament has some kind of tangible reality attached to it.

Just as He became a man so that we could see, hear, and touch Him, so He gives us enduring signs of His presence and His grace that we can see and touch.

There's an important reason for these signs. We are physical people. We live in the physical world—a world of sights and smells and objects. In the sacraments, the life of God comes to us. When He comes to us, He comes on our terms. Just as He became a man so that we could see, hear, and touch Him, so He gives us enduring signs of His presence and His grace that we can see and touch. In the sacraments, ordinary substances like bread, wine, and water take on extraordinary significance. Those substances—the bread, water, and wine—aren't there just as symbols of something we can't see. They are a part of the process, a part of the sacrament. Sacraments are where divine, intangible realities meet our human, tangible world. They are God's way of becoming visibly present to us.

We're going to talk about five of the sacraments in the next few chapters. Confirmation is the "sacrament of evangelization" and should be discussed in that context, so we will discuss that sacrament later. The final sacrament, anointing of the sick, is a sacrament of strength, grace, and healing for those who are aged or seriously ill. It's an important sacrament, but not generally discussed in the Holy Father's World Youth Day addresses, so we won't discuss it much here, either.

These chapters are intended to reacquaint you, through the words of John Paul II, with divine realities that may have already occurred, and may still be occurring, in your own lives, as well as to prepare you for decisions and sacred events in your future. Don't go through these events by rote. Understand and treasure them. Through them, God is reaching out to you in an extraordinary way.

6

Does Baptism Really Matter?

At some point Christ entered your lives and invited you to a greater awareness of your baptismal consecration; with God's grace and the help of a believing community you grew in understanding of your Christian identity and your role in the Church and society.

— John Paul II, Denver, 1993

The new life which exists in you by reason of baptism is the source of your Christian hope and optimism.

— John Paul II, Manila, 1995

I don't remember anything about when *I* was baptized, but I do remember my second brother's baptism. I was five at the time, and he was basically zero. Actually, I think he was probably about a week old. A few days before-hand, I had asked my parents what baptism was, and they told me that it was cleansing him of original sin. From that point on, I figured he was lying in his bassinet, thinking evil thoughts about how he wanted to kill everybody. I wanted to get on with the baptism before he got big enough to do anything about it. I was relieved afterward, figuring that, now he was filled with the Holy

Spirit, he must be thinking nice loving thoughts about how wonderful everybody was.

Okay, so my theology was a little flawed. I was only five. But I think that today, a lot of people older than five lack a real understanding of what the sacrament of baptism is. They see it as an excuse to get their friends together after the baby's born. They see it as a rite of passage, like a bar mitzvah. Sometimes they don't see it as much at all, and they don't get around to doing it until the "baby" can practically drive himself to the church.

Baptism is a big deal. It's important—fundamentally important—to our relationship with God. It's the first and primary sacrament. It's the "ground floor" of life in Christ. It's our "ticket" into that great, protective Church we talked about.

The need for baptism goes back to Adam and Eve. The "story" of Adam and Eve may have happened as the book of Genesis describes it, what with the snake and the fruit and the fig leaves and all. Maybe it didn't happen exactly like that. But what it does tell us, from a theological point of view, is that from the very beginning, man disobeyed God and caused a fundamental rupture in our relationship with Him. We have, as a result of that disobedience, a natural tendency to sin. There exists a great chasm between God and us, between our world and His.

We've all seen that rupture, in our lives and in the lives of those around us. We've seen that people can tend toward evil. We've noticed that societies need to be policed to keep people in line. We've noticed that, left to our own devices, selfishness can be a lot more attractive to us than selfless giving.

That rupture, that chasm, was the reason Christ came into the world in the first place. He came to repair the damage, to reconcile the world to God. He knew that we were miserable—in the long run, we can't be anything *but* miserable without God. He didn't want us to be miserable, so He came to fix things.

But how was He going to do that? Well, there are a lot of ways He *could've* done it. He could've just wiped out that tendency in everybody. Of course, He wouldn't have had to come down for that. He could have just made the adjustment from where He was, like making an ATM transfer. But that wouldn't have allowed us free will. We wouldn't love God *freely* then. We'd love Him because we were programmed to. And who wants to be loved by someone who *has* to love you? It's not genuine that way. He made us to be free. So rejecting Him has to remain an option, so that we can remain free.

But this original sin makes accepting God difficult sometimes. So He gave us help. Big help. He gave us a way to transform ourselves, to overcome that tendency to sin. "I came that you might have life, and have it abundantly." He came to show us the way, through His power and His strength, to heal the rift between us and God.

But that healing doesn't happen automatically. We need to accept it, to buy into it. God gives us the way and the power to reconcile our lives with His, but we need to act, to do it; or rather, actively to allow Him to do it—to allow Him to work in us to heal the rift.

This sounds exactly like the kind of help we need. When the chips are down, we need that help more than anything else—because reconciling with God is all that matters in the end. It's the only way we can be *really* happy—in this life or in the next.

So how do we get this help? We know He founded a Church and that He stays with her. We know that the power to reconcile must have something to do with that Church. We know the Church is His instrument of salvation. But how do we tap into that power and that protection. Do we have to join? Pay dues? Go through an orientation seminar? Is it enough just to show up?

"Go therefore and make disciples of all nations, baptizing them in the name of the Father and of the Son and of the Holy Spirit" (Mt 28:19). The key to accessing God's power, the key to getting onto God's side of the chasm, is the sacrament of baptism. It places us squarely in the middle of His Church, His instrument of salvation. It puts us on the path to sanctity. It erases the past (all seven days of it, in my brother's case, plus the nine months he spent *in utero*, where his opportunity to commit sins was somewhat limited). It gives us access to the power, won by Christ on the Cross, that makes union with God possible. It makes us new creations in Christ. It's the first step to abundant life. It gives us "hope and optimism".

So why do we baptize little babies? Are they choosing God? No, but without help, how will they? Baptism is no guarantee that children will grow up loving God and living holy lives. But baptism places them on the right side of the chasm where they can have the help, the grace, that they need to choose Him. Those choices don't start when they are ten or twelve. They start when a child decides to obey or disobey, or whether or not to share.

A couple of weeks ago, I overheard a couple of my friends' three-year-old daughters talking to each other after Mass. Their conversation went something like this: "I don't like the devil." "Me neither." "But I like Jesus a lot." "Me too."

That's where the life of faith starts.

Children need to begin to learn about God early, and

they need the grace of baptism to do that well. Union with God is not just for grown-ups. Christ said, "Suffer the little children to come unto me." He wants them to be joined with Him.

And besides, not all babies grow up to be adults. Some don't live that long. We want to place them on the right side, right away. Baptism places them in the Church, God's instrument of salvation, from the start. And there's no better way to start.

So when John Paul II wants to inspire the youth, he doesn't refer to some "new" inspiration happening in their lives. He points back to an old one, the original one. When Christ enters our lives and speaks to us, He's drawing back on that first time He entered our lives—baptism. The Holy Father urges us to draw on those graces, with the help of the believing community, and to find hope and optimism there. Whenever we do good, whenever we participate in the Church, whenever we grow in holiness, we are acting on the graces of our baptism.

Do you act on the graces of your baptism? Do you ever stop to think about how lucky you are to have been baptized? Do you ever reaffirm that baptismal commitment to God? And most important, do you work to *stay* on the side of the chasm that baptism put you on? Baptism gave you a tremendous grace, a tremendous power to repair a rift that could never heal any other way.

Don't forget those graces. Don't take them for granted. And, most important, don't lose them. You never know when you may need them.

7

Why Bother Going to Confession?

In that silence, may inner peace come to you, a peace which can be deepened and more fully possessed through the sacrament of reconciliation. . . . I hope you will avail yourselves of the many priests who are here. In the sacrament of penance they are ambassadors to you of Christ's loving forgiveness.

— *John Paul II, Denver, 1993*

Have you ever prayed and felt nothing? Stupid question, I know. Everyone who's persisted in any kind of prayer life has had times when an encounter with God didn't register on the emotional level. That's normal. Our relationship with God isn't just about emotion. No relationship is. Feelings come and go. They're dependent on how our day is going, how we're feeling, what we ate for breakfast, and various hormonally induced factors. God isn't some feeling factory where we "plug in" and automatically attain peace.

But what's going on when you *constantly* feel empty in God's presence? What's happening when you don't feel connected to Him, or when you feel vaguely uncomfortable around Him? Why is it that sometimes you look for that peace, but it never seems to come?

When this happens, it's time to take a good look at yourself. How important has God been in your life? Are you trying to live a relationship with Him and get all the spiritual benefits (inner peace, etc.) without "picking up the cross"? Do you want to have God on your own terms—only when you're in trouble or needing a shot of peaceful easy feeling, while the rest of the time you live by your own rules instead of His?

Is there unrepented sin in your life?

When the relationship is off, the peace is off. You're not comfortable together. That's what happens in God's presence when we sin.

Put it in terms of a human relationship. Say you're dating someone. At first, you feel this wonderful sense of security and bliss when you're together. You love to take long walks, just holding hands and being together. But then this person does something to hurt you—bad. It happens several times. There's never an apology, never any indication that the hurtful behavior will stop. Then suddenly this person wants to take one of those nice long walks. Will there be that same feeling of peace? No way. The relationship has been violated. You're not the same together. The peace wasn't magic—it was a function of the relationship. When the relationship is off, the peace is off. You're not comfortable together.

That's what happens in God's presence when we sin. We're not comfortable with Him any more. We don't want to look at Him too closely, and we certainly don't want Him looking too closely at us. Even if we don't consciously realize that's the problem, it's there.

We can't have peace with God if we plan to keep hurting Him, whether it's by being cruel and uncharitable to people around us or by ignoring His standard for sexuality, or whatever. The relationship doesn't work that way.

How do we make it right again? Well, how would it work in the example? The offender would have to come clean and say, "I'm sorry I hurt you, I love you, and I promise to try really hard not to do it again." *Then* you could talk it out and rebuild trust in each other, so once again you could have those nice, peaceful walks.

It works the same with God. If we want the peace He gives, the peace the world can't give, we have to walk with Him. All the way. And that walk involves a cross. It's not easy to avoid sin, but it's a part of the bargain, a part of our relationship with Him.

In a human relationship, there are different ways to hurt someone, different levels of violation of friendship. You could say something mean about someone. Or you could murder that person's family. Obviously the second would be a much bigger violation of the friendship than the first. It would probably rupture your friendship forever.

It's the same in our relationship with God. There are smaller sins and more serious ones. The smaller sins are called venial sins. Most of the sins that people commit frequently—using bad language, telling "little white lies", etc.—are venial sins. Venial sins "chip away" at our relationship with God, but they don't, by themselves, sever it.

Some sins, on the other hand, are big sins. Stealing, murder, destroying someone's life or reputation, sex outside of marriage—those offend God a lot. (Sex? *Really?* You'll see why soon.) These big sins are called mortal sins. To know something is a mortal sin and freely choose to do it anyway is to cut ourselves off from God. Mortal sins sever our relationship with Him. That's a bad position to be in, especially if you happen to die. Then God is all you have left, and you *don't* want to be cut off from Him. Your eternal life is at stake.

Obviously we need to root all mortal sin from our lives. But we need to get rid of venial sins, too. After all, when you're trying to be a good friend to someone, is it enough not to murder his family? No. You need to strive constantly to be good to him, in the little ways as well as the big. Killing someone's mother will ruin your friendship. But constantly lying to him will eventually do the same thing.

If we want to have the peace Christ gives, we have to root out sin, mortal and venial, from our lives. There's no other way. Sometimes that's not easy. We have to determine if our behavior is sinful—and if it is, we have to stop. We have to respect God's law. We have to be examples of His love. And when we fail to live up to that, which we all do sometimes, we can't run away from our failure. We have to face up to it, repent, and move on.

Have you ever heard someone say, "What I've done is so bad, even God couldn't forgive me." If you murder your friend's family, odds are you'll never get that friendship back, no matter how sincerely you apologize. God, on the other hand, *always* forgives. No matter what we've done, no matter how awful it seems, if we say to Him, "I'm so sorry. I wish I hadn't done it, and I'm committed to trying very hard not to do it again", He takes us back.

I want to say that again, because many people miss this point. *No matter what we've done, God always forgives us if we're truly sorry.* We just have to go to Him and ask.

"Going to Him" is a little harder to do than going to a person, because we can't see Him. With friends, we can look at them and hear them and work with them. They hear our apologies, and we hear them forgive. It helps the healing.

God knew we needed that, so He gave us a way. The sacrament of penance. Confession. We can actually go somewhere and hear the voice of someone assigned and called by Christ, who tells us that our sins are forgiven.

Confession restores our relationship with God. If we've committed venial sins, confession repairs the damage. And if we've committed mortal sins, confession reconnects the severed relationship.

The sacrament of penance is the system Christ gave us for the forgiveness of sins. It's the only system He gave us. He told the apostles, "If you forgive the sins of any, they are forgiven them. If you retain them, they are retained" (Jn 20:22–23). In other words, priests have Christ's sacramental power to forgive sins, and they do that in the confessional.

Christ knew what He was doing when He gave us the sacrament of penance. Like all the other sacraments, confession is a physical act. He gave us a place to go, where we can "leave" our sins and take grace in their place. He gave us a place where we have someone to talk to if we have questions—someone who doesn't even necessarily know who we are. God knows that, as human persons, we operate on the physical level. In something as important as forgiveness, He wants it to operate on the tangible level. He wants us to be there, to go to it, to hear it.

I know it's easy to want to avoid the confessional. You're afraid the priest may recognize your voice. It takes effort. It may be a little scary. It's a lot easier just to whisper in the dark, "God, I'm sorry."

Don't be afraid of the confessional. Go regularly. You don't have to go face to face. The priest doesn't have to know who you are. But you don't have to be *afraid* of going face to face either. You're not going to shock him. He hears this stuff all the time. He, better than anyone, knows that we're all human. And he won't tell anyone. He can't. Even under the threat of death, he can't reveal what's been said in the confessional. Your secret is safe with him.

But he will tell *you* something. He'll say, "I absolve you from your sins." You'll know it, because Christ said it was true. That priest isn't just some guy. He's a guy acting for Christ. He's the "ambassador of Christ's loving forgiveness".

And the relationship will be back. The peace will be back. All will be right between you and God.

Nothing is better than that.

8

We Don't Really *Eat* Christ's Body. Or Do We?

Through the sacraments, especially penance and the Eucharist . . . you have had a real and transforming experience of the new life which only Christ can give.

— *John Paul II, Denver, 1993*

It's easy to go to Mass on auto pilot. You genuflect, go into the pew, sit down, stand up, kneel, mumble the prayers, think about your girlfriend or your plans for the afternoon, mumble more prayers, stand again, shake someone's hand, kneel, get up, walk up the aisle, receive the body and blood of Christ. . . .

Hey, wait a minute! Receive the *body of Christ*? Take the actual flesh of Jesus Christ into your mouth, down your throat, and into your digestive system? Eat the flesh of a Guy who lived two thousand years ago? You do that? And you do it without even thinking about it?

Maybe it's time to do a little thinking. *Do* you do that? Do you believe that's what you're doing? Do you think about what you're doing? Or is communion just another part of the Mass for you? Do you take it seriously, or is it just one more hoop to jump through before you get to go home and talk on the phone?

A lot of Catholics aren't too clear on this whole concept of the Eucharist. They're not too sure what it is. We don't *really* believe it's the actual body and blood of Christ, do we? It's just a symbolic thing, right? A meal, right? I mean, otherwise it'd be too gross even to think about, much less do.

Guess again. The Church *does* believe that the Eucharist is the real body and blood of Christ. We believe that after the words of consecration ("This is My body . . ." and "This is My blood . . ."), the bread and wine are no longer bread and wine. They've become Jesus Christ, body, blood, soul, and divinity. He's there.

How did we come up with *this* one? Did a bunch of bishops get together at some point? ("Hey, guys, here's a good one. We'll make them believe that *wine* becomes *blood*. That'll freak them out!") No. We don't need to make this stuff up. Like everything else, we believe it because Christ told us it's true. He told us in no uncertain terms.

How it all happened is described in the Gospels. John tells us Jesus was teaching His disciples, talking about bread. And He said something really astounding. He said, "Truly, truly I say to you, unless you eat the flesh of the Son of Man and drink His blood, you have no life in you . . . for my flesh is real food indeed and my blood is real drink indeed" (Jn 6:53–55). He was pretty adamant on the point and repeated it a whole lot of different ways. You should read the whole chapter. It's really quite good.

The disciples figured He didn't really mean it. They asked for clarification. And again, He insisted He meant it. Literally. "Real food indeed. Real drink indeed."

They should've known when He said, "truly, truly". He wasn't fooling around.

Naturally, they freaked out. Following Jesus was one thing. Living the commandments was fine. Loving your neighbor was nice. But cannibalism wasn't really their gig. "After this many of his disciples drew back and no longer went about with Him" (Jn 6:66). He lost a lot of support. But he didn't try to get them back. He never said, "Come on, guys! I didn't really mean it! It's just symbolic." He let them go. And Christ hated to see people go. He wouldn't have let that happen over a misunderstanding. He meant what He said.

So how do we get this bread that gives us eternal life, the bread that is really His body? He told us that, too, at the Last Supper. "And He took bread, and when He had given thanks He broke it and gave it to them, saying, 'This is my body which is given for you. Do this in remembrance of me.' And likewise the cup after supper, saying, 'This cup which is poured out for you is the new covenant in my blood'" (Lk 22:19-20).

Christ made things pretty clear. Unless we eat His flesh, we have no life within us. Receiving the Eucharist is a big deal. It's important. It's essential to our life in Him. It's essential to our staying on the right side of the big gap between God and man.

It's a pretty awesome thing, when you think about it. God, the big God, the God of Abraham, Isaac, and Jacob, the God who created the universe and holds it in existence—*He* comes into you in a very real, very physical way. He becomes tangibly present in your body. He gets as close to you as He possibly can.

When you understand that, you get a little better understanding of people who go to Mass every day.

They're not going just to sit down, stand up, mumble prayers, and kneel. They're going to receive the body, blood, soul, and divinity of Christ. They're going to drink Him into their lives, literally, so that He remains present to them. They're going so that, with Him constantly present, they'll be better able to love as He loves. They'll be stronger Christians and live better lives. They're going to receive grace. They don't go because they're really good people. At least that's not why I go. I go because I'm not always such a great person, and I need a lot of help.

All of this tells us something about how we should approach communion. He said, "Do this in remembrance of Me." Not "Do this thinking about your weekend", or "Do this without paying attention." Receiving the Eucharist is a profound act. It's as close as you'll get to God in this life. If we want to receive all the benefit we can from it, we need to have the right attitude. Our approach needs to be prayerful, respectful, and reverent.

Receiving the Eucharist is a profound act. It's as close as you'll get to God in this life.

We also need to approach the Eucharist "clean". We just can't sin all week and then expect to receive the body and blood of Christ. It doesn't work that way. Receiving the Eucharist worthily means going to Him with a clear conscience. If you've committed a *serious* sin you haven't confessed, to go to communion would be another serious sin. It's a "slap in the face" to God. It's trying to have it both ways, and it doesn't work. Far from strengthening your faith, receiving communion unworthily will diminish it. A man named Voltaire once said that the surest way to lose your faith is to commit a mortal sin and then go to communion. It's a "grace drain", it's really, really wrong, and it's jeopardizing your immortal soul.

So the Eucharist is serious business. It's the best thing we have going in our day-to-day life—constant, ongoing contact with the Living God. It's our "daily bread" that nourishes us in our spiritual life. It provides us with our USRDA of grace.

Don't take the Eucharist lightly. Think about what you're doing. Pay attention to the consecration at Mass. Something really incredible is happening up there—be a part of it. And don't settle for "starvation rations". Receive the Eucharist as often as you can and as worthily as you can. It's your spiritual food, and the more you get, the richer your spiritual life will be.

9

What Does the Church *Really* Say about Sex and Marriage?

Be free from so many slaveries, such as sexual disorders. . . .

— John Paul II, Buenos Aires, 1987

How many . . . think that because certain forms of behavior are socially accepted they are therefore morally right? They abuse the beautiful gift of sexuality. . . .

— John Paul II, Manila, 1995

I appeal especially to young people to rediscover the wealth of wisdom, the integrity of conscience and the deep interior joy which flow from respect for human sexuality understood as a great gift from God and lived according to the truth of the body's nuptial meaning.

— John Paul II, Denver, 1993

When most people think of the Catholic Church's teaching on sex and marriage, they don't think anything particularly positive. They've probably heard some vague rumors that the Church teaches that sex outside marriage is a sin. They probably *haven't* heard a very good explanation of *why* the Church would teach something like that, especially in this day and age. I mean, face it, these days sex is presented as the best thing that will ever happen to us, and it's used to sell everything from toothpaste to tires. A lot of people think the Church must be hopelessly backward and repressed to restrict something so important.

Well, these people haven't met John Paul II.

"The nuptial meaning of the body" is a phrase from his "Theology of the Body". For those of you who weren't around or weren't reading the papers in the late seventies and early eighties, I'll explain. Every Wednesday, the Pope gives what are known as the "Wednesday audiences"—talks in St. Peter's Square addressed to whatever tourists and little old Italian ladies and international journalists might be listening.

Most popes spent this time talking about the state of the Church or general ways to be holy, or things like that. Not this Pope. He spent the first five years talking about —you guessed it—sex and marriage. Yes, this Pope knew that there was a lot of confusion among Catholics, and that a lot of it was centered around issues of sexuality. So he used the Wednesday audiences to help clear things up.

What does a pope say about sex for five straight years? "Don't do it don't do it don't do it don't do it"? Hardly. His goal wasn't *just* to tell us to wait until marriage. He wanted us, and still wants us, to understand the *beauty* of sex in God's creation and how it relates to the sacrament of marriage. He wants us to understand that God created sex and that He created it to express a certain meaning and a certain language. He wants us to see sex as a "great gift from God" and to live the *truth* of our bodies. He wants us to have the "deep interior joy" that results, not just from saying No, but from understanding *why* we're saying it—a joy that comes from realizing our No is only part of a much larger Yes to God's plan. To do that, John Paul II starts by going back to Genesis, back to creation, when God created sex and marriage.

In the story of creation in Genesis, God said after creating Adam, "It is not good for man to be alone." He wasn't just talking about Adam. He was talking about us, too. We weren't made to go through life alone. We were made to live our lives, not just for ourselves, but for and with other people. When we try to live in our own little isolated islands of ourselves, we get very lonely and bitter. It doesn't work. We want to intertwine our lives with other people's lives. We want to go beyond ourselves. We want to exist in someone else's orbit, not just our own.

So God created Eve. And Adam said, "This at last is bone of my bones and flesh of my flesh." He saw, for the first time, another person, another way of being human. He saw an equal, someone like him with whom he could share his life. He saw someone he could care about more than himself. Adam and Eve both existed so that each would have something bigger than themselves to live for. They were made to live for the good of the other and for the good of the community they formed. They were made to find their fulfillment in caring about each other.

Then there comes an interesting phrase. "The man and his wife were naked and not ashamed." How'd they do that? Did they just have really great bodies? And isn't that wrong anyway? I mean, that's what *Playboy* says. Why could they be "naked and not ashamed", but we can't?

The reason Adam and Eve could do this was because, before original sin, they could totally *trust* each other. It says "the man and his wife". Adam and Eve were married, in the best of all possible marriages. They were *totally* committed to each other (although they didn't really have much choice, I guess. It's not as if he could run off with his secretary or anything.) They were *totally trustworthy* to each other. Adam's *only* interest was what was best for Eve, and Eve's only interest was what was best for Adam. And they both knew that. Eve knew she could trust Adam completely. She knew that he'd never use her. And vice versa. It was *easy* for Eve to live totally for Adam, because she knew he was totally living for her, too, so he'd never "take advantage" of her generosity. People were like that—before original sin.

Adam and Eve had a great marriage.

Our bodies aren't just lumps of flesh that our souls ride around in.

Sex, then, between the first husband and wife, was more than just a way to feel good. It was an extension and a symbol of this total love and trust they had for each other. In giving their bodies to each other, they were really giving *themselves* to each other. They were saying, "I am yours. I am totally at your service. I give myself to you, and to your good and the good of our family, for the rest of my life." And through that act of loving self-gift, they cooperate with God in His favorite act, bringing *new* life into the world.

That is the "nuptial meaning of the body". It says that our bodies aren't just lumps of flesh that our souls ride around in. Our bodies are *ourselves*, and they express the inner person to the outer world. The body and its actions have meaning; they have a language. Nowhere is that more true than in the realm of sexual expression.

God designed sex to say something—to say, "I give myself to you forever, and I dedicate myself to what's best for you—forever." It doesn't mean, "I give myself to you for now, but I may take myself back later." or "I'm doing this 'cause it feels good for me, so don't get too attached." The body has a meaning, a nuptial meaning, and the heart knows that. Sexual expression says forever—it says marriage. It did then, and it still does today.

Wouldn't that be nice? To have someone in your life who was committed to you forever and who really did want what was best for you? Someone you could totally trust not to flake out on you, not to be hurtful or cruel to you, not to manipulate you—someone who would totally accept you and love you no matter what? In that kind of environment, *you'd* be free to love totally and to give yourself to that other person unconditionally, because you'd know he'd never take advantage of it. You could open up, because you wouldn't have to hide or protect yourself. You could act totally for your spouse's good, secure in the knowledge that someone was looking out for your good—that same spouse. And sex would be so *awesome*. "Deep interior joy" is an understatement. Sex with someone you knew would *never* leave you, *never* use you, and *never* hurt you would be an expression of pure love and trust.

That's sex the way it's supposed to be. That's marriage the way it's supposed to be. That's the truth about the body—the nuptial meaning of the body that John Paul II was talking about.

This is why the Church teaches that marriage is forever. It's not just a tough "rule". It's not a rule at all; it's just a description. All the Church is saying is that marriage isn't just about two people. It's about two people and God. In the sacrament of marriage, God does more than change their names. He binds them together spiritually. He binds their souls together. And He binds with a glue that was never meant to be unstuck. The Church doesn't allow divorces because God never gave us the authority to allow them. He said, "Everyone who divorces his wife and marries another makes her an adulteress . . ." (Mt 5:32).

Teens always ask me, "What about an annulment? Isn't that just the Catholic version of divorce?" No. An annulment doesn't say that a couple used to be married and now they're not. In an annulment, the Church looks at what was going on at the time of the wedding, to see if there was something going on that would have prevented the sacrament of marriage from taking place. If one of the partners didn't intend to consent to a permanent, faithful marriage that was open to new life, then what happened there that day wasn't a marriage, and no spiritual bond could have taken place. An annulment just acknowledges that fact, it doesn't change any facts, and it doesn't break a bond.

Of course, if things had stayed the same between Adam and Eve, we wouldn't need to be worrying about divorces at all. Their love was too pure and their trust too complete for them to have problems like that. But all good things seem to come to an end, and so it was with this state of original purity that made it so easy for Adam and

Eve to love each other. The snake showed up, Eve ate the fruit, and life got a little tougher for all of us. But what does this mean for the rest of us? What about our nuptial meaning of the body? Does love triumph in the end? Can the sacrament of marriage survive?

After the Fall—Loving Turns to Using

Original sin had a profound effect on male/female relationships, and that effect goes beyond the realm of sex. It affects everyone who is dating, whether we're sexually involved or not. And it affects people after they're married.

After the Fall, God said something very interesting to Eve. He said, "Your desire shall be for your husband, and he shall lord it over you." In other words, Eve will want that total unity and trust that they had before the Fall. But it'll be tougher for her to get it, because Adam's temptation will be to use Eve's desire for unity to get something for himself, like sex or attention.

After Adam and Eve sinned, the first thing Adam said to God was "I hid because I was naked." How did he suddenly know he was naked? Before, he was "naked and not ashamed". Did he suddenly just "notice"? Was his body different? Did he suddenly develop cellulite or a beer belly?

No. Adam's body didn't change. But something inside him changed. Before, he was totally dedicated to what was best for Eve, and his body was an expression of that. But now his attitude toward Eve is different. He realizes he doesn't *have* to look out for what is best for her. If he's not quite so concerned about what happens to Eve, he can look out for himself. For the first time, he's figured out that he can *use* Eve just to make himself feel good. And Eve has figured out the same thing about Adam. This using is sin. For Adam and Eve, it's a new concept.

Trouble is, each one has figured out that the *other* has figured it out, too. Trust is out the window. Eve knows Adam might use her, and vice versa. They both may want to use each other, but neither wants to *be* used. So they are protecting themselves—hiding, ashamed of using and afraid of being used.

The party's over.

Sound a lot like life today? It should. Remember, this is about us, not just Adam and Eve. Their sin affects all of us, in the form of this original sin problem we discussed earlier. Because of original sin, we're inclined to be selfish—to use each other and just look out for ourselves. Because of that, we have a tough time trusting each other, and an even tougher time getting along with each other.

It can be really tempting to use people. Sometimes we do it without even thinking about it.

This lack of trust, and the inclination to use other people, affects all areas of our lives, but perhaps none so intimately and devastatingly as sex and relationships between men and women. We want to love, and we want to be loved. But, because of the tendency to sin we inherited from Adam and Eve, we are tempted to use. We start to believe that we can get some good stuff for ourselves if we just try not to care who gets hurt.

It can be really tempting to want to use people. Sometimes we do it without even thinking about it. Everyone else has a date? Better be nice to the one guy who might ask you. You're not necessarily interested in him, but you want to go someplace nice for dinner. All the other guys have girlfriends? That girl likes you, and she's really beautiful. Of course, she's dumb and she gets on your nerves, but you could flatter her if you had to. It'd be worth it for the guys to see you with a hot babe.

The other part of the problem is that we never really know when other people are thinking the same kinds of things about us. We're not sure whom to trust. Sometimes it's hard to tell if someone really cares about you, or if he's pretending because he wants to use you.

Sex hasn't changed. It still has the same meaning: "I give myself to you forever. I want what's best for you forever. I want to share new life with you." And the heart still hears all of that. But sex also feels good, and we get tempted to "say" it when we don't "mean" it—because it makes our bodies feel good, or makes us feel less alone, or makes us more popular. So we tell a lie with our bodies—we say "forever" when we don't mean it. We use someone—getting a thrill for ourselves at their expense and at the expense of their (and our) relationship with God.

This is what the second part of the Theology of the Body says—that with original sin, lust entered our hearts. Now lust doesn't mean just sexual attraction. Sexual attraction is normal. It's the way God made us. Lust means the willful desire to use someone—in this case, to use someone's body—for our own purposes or our own pleasure. It forgets that each person was created in the image and likeness of God and that God wants only what is best for that person. And He expects us to love others the same way. When we use someone—anyone—we're going against His will.

Speaking the "language of the body" outside of marriage is always a lie, always a sin, and always using another person. It goes against the "truth" of the body, its built-in language. It takes something beautiful and strips it of its meaning. It degrades a great gift. And it makes a human being, whom God loves, into just another "thing" to help us get what we want.

No one can love and use at the same time. Love requires trust, and if you believe that someone might use you, you're not going to trust that person. Where there's use, where there's lust, there is no trust. That's why respecting God's plan for sexuality is the only way to find love. If you're using someone, trust is lost. Without trust, love dies. Love wants what's best for the other, and using just doesn't fit in.

Where is "deep, interior joy" in this scenario? Using and deep joy don't generally go together. Look at the people you know who are sexually active outside marriage. Do you see joy? Do you see serenity? If you've been sexually active outside marriage, has it brought you peace? Has it brought harmony to your relationship? Has it brought trust or security?

Going outside of God's plan doesn't bring lasting joy. That's especially true when it comes to sex. God designed sex for self-giving, for permanently committed married love. And the people who are expressing it that way are, as we said, experiencing a real peace and joy—plus having an awful lot of fun.

I read an interesting study the other day. The study was

on sexual satisfaction among Americans.[1] Do you know who in America reports the very highest level of sexual satisfaction? Married people. And not just any married people, but highly religious married people who waited until they were married to have sex. So much for the stereotype that religious people think sex is dirty. They're having more fun than anyone.

It makes sense. They're doing it the way God intended it to be done. They're speaking the language honestly. They don't fear abandonment or AIDS. They can cut loose and enjoy themselves.

Do you know who in America reports the very highest level of sexual satisfaction? Married people.

But outside of His plan, sex doesn't work the same. It causes damage. It puts pressure on relationships. It reduces trust. It brings all kinds of worries—pregnancy, disease, AIDS, getting caught, being rejected. How much fun can you have when you're worried about all of that? Unmarried sex tends to cause couples to fight more. It puts too much pressure on them. Even if they're *trying* to love each other, sex isn't the way to do it. Even if they don't *mean* to use each other, they are. They're putting each other at risk of damage, and that's not loving, it's using. And we can't use someone and learn to love at the same time.

None of this means that the beautiful language of sex

[1] William Mattox, *What's Love Got to Do with It? Good Sex Comes to Those Who Wait* (Washington, D.C.: Family Research Council, 1995).

can't also be abused within marriage. It can. If one partner doesn't care about the other and sees sex only as a means of self-gratification, that person is using, not loving. And there's no place for using or lust in marriage, either. Sex should be an expression of love for the other, not just a way to have our own desires satisfied regardless of what happens to the other.

Wouldn't you rather love and be loved than use and be used? Most people would. But love is a lot tougher to find since this original sin thing makes it so easy to use each other. Is it hopeless? What can we do?

New Life—and Love—in Christ

Our capacity for love didn't disappear with sin. It was just threatened. As John Paul II says, the heart is now a "battleground" between love and lust. Each one of us is struggling to get the upper hand, to gain control of our relationships and our lives.

Since Christ, we have a new weapon in that battle. We have the graces He won for us on the Cross. St. Paul says that, in Christ, we are a "new creation". That means that, if we tap into Christ and His power, we can do things we never could have done on our own. Things like love unselfishly even when we'd rather be looking out for ourselves. Things like respect our sexuality even when the drives are incredibly strong.

Marriage is a sacrament. Like the other sacraments, it brings grace. That grace is important to marriages, and it's important to marital sex. It's the action of God in our lives that helps us to channel this really powerful sexual energy and to have the strength to use it at the service of love.

We're fools if we believe we can do anything on our own—especially something as difficult as loving. God is the author of love. He *is* love. The best way for us to respect our sexuality, and to build the best relationships we can, is to put *Him* in the driver's seat. And we do that by praying to Him constantly and, especially, by turning our relationships over to Him.

It may not seem easy at first, but the rewards are great. Rewards like "deep interior joy". Rewards like relationships that work. Rewards like a lifetime of really great married sex.

10

Whom Does God Call to Religious Life?

Bishops, priests and deacons share in Christ's ministry through the ordained ministry. Men and women religious share in it through the spousal love manifested in the spirit of the evangelical counsels of chastity, poverty and obedience.

— *John Paul II, Manila, 1995*

At a time like this . . . when there are not enough priests, not enough religious sisters and brothers to give support and guidance, not enough contemplative religious to keep before people's eyes the sense of the absolute supremacy of God, we must be convinced that Christ is knocking at many hearts, looking for people like you to send into the vineyard, where an abundant harvest is ready.

— *John Paul II, Denver, 1993*

Who becomes a priest? Who becomes a nun? I always thought of priests and nuns as different—as though they were priests and nuns when they were born. They weren't like you and me. They were set apart from the start. They didn't live normal teenage lives. They certainly weren't interested in the opposite sex. And there's

68

no way they dated or anything. *He's a priest, for Pete's sake!*

Entering the priesthood or religious life is something *other* people do, isn't it? Not something you'd think of. I mean, sure it's a great thing, I guess. They serve God, or whatever. But you? Nah. It's just for them.

What exactly does being a priest or a nun involve? What's the difference between being priests and nuns and sisters and brothers, and between all of them and the rest of us?

The Priesthood

What is a priest? Is he just a full-time "God-guy" who has made a career out of working for the Church? Is the priesthood just a "job", like being a lawyer, a chef, or a certified public accountant?

No. John Paul II says that priests "share in Christ's ministry". He does not mean this in a vague, everyone-is-supposed-to-act-like-Christ sort of way. He means it in a very specific way. The priest is an *alter Christus*, "another Christ". The *Catechism of the Catholic Church* says, "Holy Orders is the sacrament through which the mission entrusted by Christ to the apostles continues to be exercised in the Church until the end of time."[1] So the priest is, in a very real sense, a descendant of the apostles. In fact, he is ordained by a bishop, who was ordained by a bishop, who was ordained by a bishop, and so on, until you get all the way back to the *first* bishops, who were the apostles themselves. Priests continue their work.

The priest has the power to act *in persona Christi*—in

---

[1] *Catechism of the Catholic Church*, part II, section vi, no. 860.

the person of Christ. When he forgives sins, unites couples in marriage, and consecrates the sacred Host, he isn't just acting as himself, Father Whoever. He's acting for Christ, who is the only one who can forgive sins, unite couples in marriage, and change bread and wine into Himself. The priest acts in the person of Christ, with powers conferred on him by Christ.

The priesthood is not just a job. It's a sacrament. In the sacrament of holy orders, a priest receives the powers given by Christ to the apostles and the graces the priest will need to carry out his very important mission in life. That's why the priesthood is different from any other job. In receiving the sacraments of holy orders, a man changes. He becomes "a priest forever, in the order of Melchizedek". He will always be a priest. He may become an inactive priest, or a laicized priest, but he will never cease to be a priest. Holy orders are for keeps.

The Priesthood—For Men Only?

There has been much discussion recently about the Church's restriction of the priesthood to men only. Many are asking why, in a Church that regards men and women as created in the image and likeness of God, equal in dignity, are women not ordained as priests?

The answer is not that women "aren't good enough", or that we "can't handle it". It is not that one gender is better than the other, but simply that gender *matters*. When a priest stands on the altar and says "This is my body", he is acting not as himself but as Christ. And Christ was a man—he was male. The person standing in His place, *becoming* Christ, must then also be male.

Put it this way. Have you ever seen the movie *Jesus of*

Nazareth? How would you have felt about that movie if the role of Mary had been played by Arnold Schwarzenneger? Or if Julia Roberts had played Jesus? It would lose something, wouldn't it? Gender does matter.

When John Paul II wrote his apostolic letter "On Reserving Priestly Ordination to Men Alone", he didn't say that the Church could ordain women but doesn't want to. He said, quoting Pope Paul VI, "The Church does not consider herself authorized to admit women to priestly ordination."[2] In explaining, he cited the reasons given above, as well as the fact that Christ, who could have chosen anyone He wanted as apostles, chose only men. He also points out that even Mary, who was the holiest person (besides her Son, of course) ever to live, was not made an apostle. So this is not an issue of "worthiness" or "holiness".

John Paul II closed that document by saying, "I declare that the Church has no authority whatsoever to confer priestly ordination on women and that this judgment is to be definitively held by all the Church's faithful."[3] In other words, the Pope said that the topic is closed. The Church won't be ordaining women because she can't ordain women. The Church doesn't make up her own power. The Church has only the powers she receives from Christ.

Religious Life

Does this mean that there is no formal role for women in the Church? Of course not. Many women, and men, for

---

[2] John Paul II, *Ordinatio Sacerdotalis*, 2.
[3] Ibid., 4.

that matter, give their lives to God through entering what is called the "religious life".

When we speak of those in "religious life", we aren't speaking of those who pray a lot and get involved in their church. We're referring to men and women who give their lives completely to God by becoming religious sisters or brothers. In religious life, they take Christ not only as their Lord and Savior but also as their spouse, forsaking a human spouse so that they can give their lives to God and His service in a total and complete way.

They pray for you and for me. They pray for the poor. They pray for the rich. They pray for the government. They pray for the world. They're probably the only ones keeping the world afloat these days.

When men become brothers or women become sisters, they follow the example of St. Paul, who said, "The unmarried man is anxious about the affairs of the Lord; but the married man is anxious about worldly affairs, how to please his wife, and his interests are divided" (1 Cor 7:32-34). St. Paul wasn't saying that marriage is a bad thing. But marriage is very time-consuming, full of jobs and grocery lists and summer vacations and forming children to know, love, and serve God and all. St. Paul was pointing out that some people are called to renounce it, so that they can dedicate themselves completely to loving God and to loving and serving the larger community of His people on earth.

I'm sure you've seen this service in action. Religious sisters and brothers often teach in Catholic schools. They work in Catholic hospitals and social service agencies. They give of themselves by serving needs in poor neighborhoods. In fact, it seems the poorer and more run-down a neighborhood is, the more likely you will be to see Mother Teresa's white-and-blue-habited sisters cheerfully working with the children, the sick, and the neediest of families.

Some religious give themselves entirely to prayer. These contemplative orders, such as the Carmelites and the Poor Clares, live in what is known as a "cloister", where they are completely shut off from the world. They don't read the newspaper. They don't watch TV. They don't talk on the phone. They don't have visitors. They don't go out. They just pray—all day, every day. They pray for you and for me. They pray for the poor. They pray for the rich. They pray for the government. They pray for the world.

They're probably the only ones keeping the world afloat these days.

I have a good friend who renounced an extremely successful and lucrative career playing professional women's basketball to join such a cloistered order of nuns. The world couldn't believe it. There were articles about it in *Sports Illustrated* and even the *National Enquirer*. (Apparently giving up a lot of money to become a nun is as weird as being abducted by aliens or giving birth to a five-headed baby.) She doesn't leave the cloister, she doesn't make phone calls, and her family is allowed to visit only a few times a year. But she can write occasional letters. Hers to me are always joyful and hilariously funny.

She says she loves her life and her vocation, and she has never been happier.

Poverty, Chastity, and Obedience

John Paul II says, "Men and women religious share in [Christ's missions] through the spousal love manifested in the spirit of the evangelical counsels of chastity, poverty, and obedience." The astute among you will recognize that, for the most part, this is true also of priests. (The exception is diocesan priests, who take vows of chastity and obedience, but not poverty.)

Why do we ask priests and religious to take these vows? Is it because we think that money, freedom, and families are bad, so people dedicated to God shouldn't go near them? No. It's more complex than that. Money, freedom, and families are all things that can bind people. Money takes time to earn. We worry about earning it. Once we have it, we worry about how to invest it. We worry about losing it. We worry about making enough. We worry about making more. A family brings similar worries. Raising children is a tremendous responsibility. It can dictate where we live, and how we spend our time and our energy. And when we have complete freedom to go where we wish and do as we wish, we tend to make those decisions based on our own limited point of view.

Priests and religious, on the other hand, are free. They are free to spend all of their time in the service of the Lord, not having to worry about how much money they're making or whether or not they're spending time with their families. They are free to go wherever and whenever they are needed—totally at the service of their Church and their religious order.

Most important, these vows testify to the outside world that our representatives have no agenda. Priests and religious are not using their religious lives to get rich, or to attract the opposite sex, or to live the kind of lives they choose. In this era of televangelist scandals and fund-raising scams, people find that comforting. The priesthood and religious life are dedicated to serving others, not to profiting from them.

Of course, priests and religious are human beings, and they are subject to the same temptations as anyone else. And, as in the rest of society, some resist those temptations while others don't. When priests and religious do sin, the world loves to point it out—I guess it makes them feel better about their own sins. But the weakness of human nature is all the more reason for the vows of poverty, obedience, and chastity. The lifestyle those vows create tends to weed out the more selfish candidates.

Jesus Knocks

John Paul II says Jesus "knocks on hearts" looking for priests and religious. Not just any heart. Certain hearts. Hearts He knows better than we do. Hearts He knows beat in men and women who He knows would serve Him well. Hearts He made particularly capable of serving Him well.

Has He ever knocked on your heart? "I wouldn't listen. I don't want to know. I don't want to be a priest." Are you sure?

To the world, being a priest doesn't look too attractive. You can't have a high-powered corporate career. You can't collect sports cars and yachts. And, yikes, you can't collect *women*! You can't even have *one*! You have to give up sex forever! Who on earth would want to do that?

But think about it from a little different perspective. As a Christian, what's the primary goal of life? Sports cars? Money? Women? No. As big a bummer as it may seem on the surface, our goal is quite simply to serve God, saving up for that big savings account in the sky. We're looking forward to that life to come, when we'll be happy forever. There's a saying, "Whoever dies with the most toys, wins." It points out an important truth. No matter how much money or how many cars you've collected, once you're gone, it goes to the taxman.

The thing is, a lot of people realize that *before* they die. The more they collect, the emptier they feel. The world told them that all of this would make them happy, but it doesn't. These *things* just sit there, and they don't bring fulfillment. They don't move us one bit closer to that final destination—the life that lasts forever.

But think of someone who lives this life with one foot in the next. Someone who's working day and night toward something that isn't going to go to the taxman in the end, but that's going to follow him into heaven. If heaven is happiness with God forever, then serving Him and helping other people get there has to be pretty rewarding work.

I know living for the next life seems kind of like a "necessary evil", like saving up your money for something you want in the future but having to suffer now and not buy anything you like. But look at the priests and sisters you know. Do they look as if they're suffering? Do they seem miserable?

Ironically, those who work for God are the ones who often find the most happiness in this life. Why? Because

God is love. And love is what we're all looking for. More than yachts, more than bucks, more than sex. And it follows that, by leading other people to Him, we're leading them to what they want most, real love in their lives. And that can't help but rub off on us.

This is an age that is starved for God, starved for love. And God needs people to be His full-time hands and feet, leading them back to Him. So He knocks. He knocks on the hearts He wants to help Him.

Is He knocking on yours? "No, he couldn't be. I like girls." Do you think God would like to have priests who dislike women, or nuns who dislike men? They wouldn't be very good priests or nuns, would they?

This is an age that is starved for God, starved for love. And God needs people to be His full-time hands and feet, leading them back to Him. So He knocks. He knocks on the hearts He wants to help Him.

A lot of priests and nuns have told me that, when they were young, they had a suspicion that God was calling them to the priesthood or religious life, but they resisted because they wanted to get married. But when they finally fell in love, they knew they had to enter religious life. Even though they had found the perfect person, the person they would want to marry, they knew something still wasn't right. They heard the knocking. It was louder than ever. They couldn't ignore it. Romance and true love couldn't quench it. God created them for Himself alone in a unique way, and He made sure they'd be satisfied only with Him. None of them has ever regretted it for a minute. (Although one did mention that he wishes God had called him "before I spent all of that time and money"!)

When God calls us to do something, He gives a certain desire for what He's called us to. He wants us to be happy, and He made us to be happy at the vocation to which He called us. Priests don't say, "Oh, man, I have to be a priest. Bummer!" There are things to renounce of course, like the yachts. But once we let go and trust Him, He often gives a joy and a peace beyond comprehension. His vineyard is important to Him. He rewards those who tend it, in this life and in the next.

Does embracing God in this way mean renouncing human love? Does it mean renouncing family? Look at the priests and nuns you know. The ones I know are surrounded by people who love them. They have *lots* of families. The fact that they've renounced exclusive love and having one family hasn't shrunk their love but multiplied it for everyone. They often live lives of incredible love.

A lot of people seem to think that priests and nuns have somehow to "repress" their sexuality. This is not an accurate understanding of celibate life. Celibacy isn't about suppressing sexual energy. That energy is there, it's a part of who we are, and it's a good thing. Celibacy is about consecrating our sexuality to *God*, giving it and our sexual energy to Him and to His service. In celibacy, we take our sexual energy and rechannel it—using that energy to express intense but nonsexual love for God and, through Him, to a whole lot of His people. Marital love uses sexual energy to express exclusive, sexual love between two people. Celibate love uses sexual energy to express inclusive, nonsexual love to everyone. Celibacy doesn't reduce love, it multiplies it.

The great Archbishop Fulton Sheen once said, "Celibacy is the hardest when we fall out of love with Christ . . . once we see it in relation to Christ, then it is less a problem and more a matter of love. Celibacy is not the absence of a passion; it is rather the intensity of a passion."[4] (Archbishop Sheen, as a matter of fact, was an amazing man who had a lot of insightful things to say. I highly recommend his autobiography, *Treasure in Clay*.)

Like every sacrament, the sacrament of holy orders brings special graces to the person who receives it. Sure it's sometimes difficult for the priest to abstain from sexual activity. That is difficult for anyone. But the grace of the sacrament helps him to fulfill his vows and to live his celibacy as a gift for God.

So the priesthood and religious life, contrary to popular belief, are not about renouncing love. Neither are they about renouncing happiness or fulfillment. They're about finding all of that, in this life and in the next, by living with one foot in this world and one foot in the next. A religious vocation isn't for everyone, of course. It's for those God calls to it, those He knows are suited for it, those who have what it takes.

When you're deciding what to do with your life, don't just automatically shut out the possibility of a religious vocation. Try to remain open to *whatever* God has in store for you. Ask for help. Pray for His guidance.

And listen for a little knocking sound.

---

[4] Fulton Sheen, *Treasure in Clay* (San Francisco: Ignatius Press, 1993), pp. 204–5.

I I

What about Other Christians?

Most of you are members of the Catholic Church; but others are from other Christian churches and communities, and I greet each one with sincere friendship. In spite of divisions among Christians, "all those justified by faith through baptism are incorporated into Christ . . . brothers and sisters in the Lord." Every meeting between young Catholics and other young Christians must be one of discovering ever more fully the riches of the gospel message together.

— *John Paul II, Denver, 1993*

We've learned all kinds of things about *our* Church—the Catholic Church. We've seen that she was founded by Jesus Christ, that He is staying close to us, and that He left us all kinds of great sacramental ways to stay close to Him.

But what do we tell our friends who belong to other Christian churches, our Protestant friends? "Sorry, Christ isn't in your church, He's in *my* church"? No. What about "Well, all churches are really pretty much the same, as long as you believe in Christ"? Not quite. It's all a little trickier than that.

For the first one thousand years or so of Christianity, people didn't have this problem. The Catholic Church was the only Christian church—the only game in town.

When disagreements about doctrine came up, the Church would hold a council where the pope, bishops, and theologians would pray and talk through the problem. They would reach a conclusion, and most everyone would respect it, believing that Christ stays with His Church.

However, in 1054 came the Great East–West Schism, when the Eastern (Orthodox) churches broke away from Rome in a dispute over the authority of the pope. Five hundred years later, bigger cracks started showing up. Martin Luther disagreed with some *essential* doctrines, and he didn't want to hang around to settle things with the Church. So he started his own church, the Lutheran church. Henry VIII of England likewise developed some theological doubts based on the fact that he wanted to divorce his wife and marry his mistress. The Church wouldn't let him, so he started his own church, the Anglican church.

Once people got the idea that they could just form their own church if they encountered conflict, it didn't stop with those two churches. People split off from them, and off from those splits, until today we have over twenty-five thousand different Protestant denominations. Christianity is very divided. Both Catholics and Protestants realize that this division is not a good thing.

There have been efforts lately to address some of those divisions. There have been "ecumenical" events and meetings, where leaders of different Christian churches get together to talk or worship. That is good. But there is a more powerful ecumenical movement growing up from the grass roots. Devout Catholics and devout Protestants, especially Evangelical Christians, are noticing that we have a lot in common, living together in a world that doesn't respect the gospel message at all. As we Catholics stand up for our Christian values, we're finding ourselves side by side with our Protestant brothers and sisters. And we're learning about each other and learning to talk about our common ground and our differences in the process.

What should our attitude be toward our Protestant friends? Well, first of all, it should be one of genuine friendship and love.

I've found this to be particularly true in the pro-life movement. Some of the most impressive, dedicated, hardworking leaders I've met have been Evangelical Christians. And I've learned a lot from their example. I've seen how they *really* put Christ first in their lives. I've seen their complete faith in Him. I've seen how completely they immerse their lives in prayer. I've seen them really get out there and try to make a difference, whereas some Catholics tend to sit back and wait for the priests to do all of the work.

What should our attitude be toward our Protestant friends? Well, first of all, it should be one of genuine friendship and love. Remember, we're all followers of the same Christ, and we're all created in His image and likeness. As the Holy Father says, they are "justified by baptism" just as we are. They are sincerely trying, just as we should be, to do God's will and to follow Him as best we can. We are, in a sense, on the road together, and we need to encourage each other and work to-gether.

As we band together, we should talk. I've found, in working with Evangelicals, that many of them have *enormous* misunderstandings about what the Catholic Church is all about. Many used to be Catholics but left the Church because they were never correctly taught about their faith, and they saw an enthusiasm and a zeal among the Evangelicals that was lacking in their own local Catholic church. Very few have an accurate understanding of what the Catholic Church is about. You can change that, by your words and by your example.

I want to encourage you to learn all you can about your faith—where it differs from the Protestant faiths, and what we have in common. Hopefully, this book should help you to understand your faith more fully. If you want to go into more depth, there are several good books out there that will help you. First and foremost, of course, is the *Catechism of the Catholic Church*. Two other excellent books on the faith are *Catholic and Christian*, by Alan Schreck, and *What Catholics Really Believe*, by Karl Keating. By being an articulate Catholic, understanding what you believe and living it out, you can be a tremendous witness to others.

It's important to work together with our Protestant friends. We follow the same Christ, and therefore we have a lot in common. And the world is largely hostile to our shared values. By all means work with them, play with them, pray with them, and commit together to "discovering ever more fully the riches of the gospel message of life and love".

But remember also that we have a tremendous treasure. We belong to the Church founded by Jesus Christ. Understand that. Rejoice in it. Be ready to explain what we believe, clearly and charitably, if you're asked.

Real friendship seeks what's best for the other. And what's best for us as Christians is understanding and unity, not confusion and division.

12

Why Do We Pray to Mary?

Mary, Mother of the Church and our mother, will help us to hear her divine Son.

— *John Paul II, Manila, 1995*

Mary, the Mother of the Redeemer, was her Son's first and best disciple. . . . She is the best guide we can have: she leads us to Christ and says: "Do whatever He tells you" (Jn 2:5).

— *John Paul II, Denver, 1993*

As Catholics, one of the most difficult aspects of our faith to explain to our Protestant friends is our relationship with Mary. We name big churches after her. We have huge feasts in her honor. We have a million prayers to her (including one particularly popular devotion involving beads, in which we pray to her no fewer than fifty times). Considering that we're dealing with a God who says, "You shall have no other gods before me", you can see where our Protestant friends might get a little suspicious. From the outside, it could look as if we've set her up as some kind of co-God.

So what's the deal with Mary? Is she a person or a God?

Or maybe someone kind of in between? Do we worship her?

Mary, as any glance at the Bible will tell us, was and is a person. She's not God, and we could no more make her God than we could make Michael Jordan into God. (I know, people have tried. It doesn't work.) She was a human being, born of two human parents. That's it.

She was, however, a particularly extraordinary human being. For one thing, she was the only human being besides her Son born without original sin. She was sinless. God made her that way for a reason. His Son was going to come into the world through her, and He wanted an appropriate "vessel".

He had another reason for creating her without original sin. She had an amazingly big job to do. She had to be the mother of God. That's right, she had to teach God how to hold His fork, and clean His room, and write His name. Try to imagine that. How do you reprimand God? Do you spank Him or bow down and worship Him? There are some pretty fine lines here. For that job, she needed all the help she could get.

Does the fact that Mary was sinless mean that she didn't need a Savior as the rest of the people around her did? Did Christ not save her? No, that's not what it means. Christ did save her. After she found out she would be the mother of Christ, she said to Elizabeth, "My spirit rejoices in God my Savior" (Lk 1:47). Mary was redeemed by Christ, just like everybody else. She was just redeemed *earlier* than the rest, so that she could act as a vessel for the Savior.

But what does all of that have to do with us? So she was sinless. She was really good at being God's mother. That's not the same as being God. What's her role in our life?

The Holy Father makes it easy to understand her role and our relationship to her. "She is the best guide we have: she leads us to Christ." She "will help us to hear her divine Son." She was the best and holiest person ever to live. She was the closest to Christ. She was "her Son's first and best disciple". She heard Him clearly and constantly. Well, what's our goal as Catholics? Our goal is to be good and holy people, to come close to Christ, to be His disciples, to hear Him. Mary, then, is a role model we can emulate. She teaches us how to follow Christ. She knows.

But she's more than just a stagnant role model whose life we can study. She's in heaven with her Son, and she can help us. Not of her own power—that would make her God. But just like people on earth can pray for us and help us, so Mary in heaven can pray for us and help us. That's what we're asking for when we pray to her: "Pray for us sinners, now and at the hour of our death. . . ."

She was the best and holiest person ever to live. She was the closest to Christ. She was "her Son's first and best disciple".

Think for a minute about Mary's role. She's God's mother. At the wedding feast at Cana, she pointed a problem out to him, and He solved it. She didn't somehow "override" Him but merely said "Do whatever He tells you." She's close to Christ. The closest. He listens to her.

Just as Mary is God's mother, so she is our mother. On the Cross, Jesus said to John, "Behold thy mother." He "gave" her to him and to all of us. She's a mother who cares about you. She knows your life and knows your trials. She's suffered, too. Her heart was "pierced by a sword" watching her Son die. She understands our suffering. And she can help, not through her own power, but through praying for us to her Son.

But Mary is more than someone who can make us feel better. She leads us to Christ. It's hard to be holy sometimes. It's hard to know how to follow Christ. But Mary knows the way. She leads us to Him.

That's Mary's role. She's not the end of the journey. She's a guide, a road map. She leads us to Christ. She's a mother who loves us and helps us through this "valley of tears".

She's your mother. Go to her.

13

What If I'm Not Sure I Believe All This Stuff?

The New Testament presents Simon—whom Jesus called Peter, the Rock—as a vigorous, passionate disciple of Christ. But he also doubted, and, at a decisive moment, he even denied that he was a follower of Jesus.

— John Paul II, Denver, 1993

Have you ever doubted?

I mean *really* doubted. Have you wondered, "Is there really a God, or am I just spinning my wheels here?" Or "What if these sacraments aren't really anything divine. Maybe they're just what they look like—bread, water, and wine." Or "What if the Bible is just a bunch of stories. Maybe there was no Christ, and there is no Church founded by Him." Or "Maybe there is a God, but it's hard to believe He cares about me, I'm miserable out here. Where are you, God?"

If you're human, I bet you've doubted at some point. Doubt is a pretty normal, human response to the prospect of basing our entire lives on Someone we can't see or touch. (At least not in recognizable form. Basing your life on Someone you *can* touch but who looks exactly like bread and wine makes people wonder sometimes, too.)

Being a Christian is a pretty life-altering experience. You have to "go against the flow" a lot. You have to do things other people don't do or refuse to do things other people do. That makes you stand out. Sometimes it's lonely. Sometimes people think you're crazy.

And you have to believe some pretty outlandish things. You have to believe that God became a man, was executed as a criminal, was dead, and then He wasn't, then rose into heaven on some kind of invisible elevator. You have to believe that He still cares about you today, even when He lets you fail a test or credit report.

So it's pretty normal once in a while to step back and say, "Wait a minute here. Is this for real?"

Of course, if you're a "good" Christian, your next response is generally, "Oh, no. I shouldn't doubt. God doesn't like that. He's probably mad at me now."

I think it's significant that the Holy Father talks about Peter. Have you ever seen the movie *Jesus of Nazareth*? Peter was the one who always looked kind of confused. His face seemed to say, "What are we *doing* here?" He'd seem as if he understood, and then he'd ask a *really* stupid question or pull a stupid stunt like denying Christ. Yet, he was the first to recognize Christ as the Messiah. And Christ chose *Peter* to lead His Church.

Doubt isn't necessarily about questioning God's existence. It's about questioning *why* we believe. That can be a good thing. It's necessary—because we believe for different reasons at different times in our lives. If you believed in God when you were a kid, it was probably because your parents told you He existed, and they read you little Bible stories with lots of big pictures. And your "prayer life" probably consisted of "Bless us, O Lord . . ." and "Now I lay me down to sleep. . . ."

Most adult Christians have hopefully moved beyond that kind of faith experience. But how does that happen? It happens when, at some point, probably as teenagers, they say, "Wait a minute. Do I believe this just because my parents said it? Is this my faith or just theirs? Is any of this true?"

There's nothing wrong with that. I think, in a way, it comes from God. It's an invitation to learn more about Him. It's an invitation to deepen our faith, to *understand* it so that we can live it more fully and share it with others. After all, it's hard to convince someone *else* of the truth of Christianity when our best argument is, "Well, my parents said it's true."

Have you ever known someone who's *really* intelligent and who questions everything? I have. I love people like that. In the short term, they can be a real pain, especially when you're talking about religion. When you answer their questions with the pat little answers you half remember from CCD, they say, "Yeah, but what about . . ." or "That doesn't quite make sense, because. . . ." They make you think a lot deeper and clarify your own faith. And intelligent people who question, and who *honestly* search for the answers, tend to become the most convinced, and the most convincing, Christians.

The problem is that some people don't take these doubts and questions as an invitation or an opportunity to learn more. They take it as an excuse to "chuck it all". Face it, a lot of people just don't *want* to live the Christian life. It's a lot easier not to be a Christian. There are a lot of sins that are awfully fun in the short run, and people who've lived in those sins for long enough no longer have the motivation to make the change or the clarity of mind they need to see God. As Scripture says, their "hearts are hardened". Their consciences have become distorted. They've been doubting and sinning for so long that they're no longer particularly interested in finding the hard answers and in making the changes those answers entail. They may discuss or argue, but it's not to find the truth—it's to justify their own lifestyle or to talk others into joining them.

So doubts aren't necessarily a bad thing. They're an invitation from God—an invitation to grow in understanding and in holiness. They're an invitation to seek and to find the truth. But we need to take them that way and really to act on them to find the answers, to find the truth. If you're doubting, and my bet is that sometimes you are, learn more. Get your questions answered. Ask your parents. Ask a priest. Go to a good Catholic bookstore and get some books on your faith. Finish reading this book. Whatever you do, get the answers.

Doubts aren't necessarily a bad thing. They're an invitation from God—an invitation to grow in understanding and in holiness.

Most important, pray. Understanding doesn't come from us, it comes from God. When Peter recognized Jesus as the Messiah, Jesus said, "Flesh and blood has not revealed this to you, but my Father who is in heaven" (Mt 16:17). *No one* who doesn't love God or have a real relationship with Him is going to "get" any of this stuff.

It just doesn't make sense from a strictly human point of view. Logic alone won't grasp it. We need the light of grace.

It's okay to doubt. It can be good—if you take it as an invitation to grow. If you're doubting, don't despair. But do go looking for the truth. Start looking now. If you let those questions ride, or if you just give in to them without searching, you're risking a spiritual "hardening of the arteries" that'll be awfully tough to correct ten years down the road.

14

How Should I "Clarify My Values"?

False teachers, many belonging to an intellectual elite in the worlds of science, culture, and the media, present an anti-gospel. . . . When you ask them, "What must I do?" their only certainty is that there is no definite truth, no sure path. They want you to be like them: doubtful and cynical. Consciously or not, they advocate an approach to life that has led millions of young people into a sad loneliness in which they are deprived of reasons for hope and are incapable of real love.

— *John Paul II, Manila, 1995*

To educate without a value system based on truth is to abandon young people to moral confusion, personal insecurity, and easy manipulation. No country, not even the most powerful, can endure if it deprives its own children of this essential good.

— *John Paul II, Denver, 1993*

Sound familiar? Educating without a value system based on truth? Sad loneliness, deprived of reasons for hope? Moral confusion, personal insecurity, easy manipulation? I don't know about you, but this sounds a lot like my high-school experience.

When was the last time you heard "truth" discussed in

a public school? I went to several different public schools, and I don't think I ever heard anything about it. Most of what I heard sounded like the "false teachers" John Paul II refers to. I heard a lot about "value systems", and about finding my own and determining what was right and wrong for me. I heard a lot about respecting other people's value systems and about the importance of not "imposing my morality" on them. But truth? Not a word. It was pretty easy to conclude that no one really knew what it was, or if it really existed at all.

That kind of attitude left a whole lot of room for "moral confusion and personal insecurity" for the rest of us. How were we supposed to figure out what our "value systems" were? On what were we supposed to base them? Are some "value systems" better than others? How could something be right for one person but wrong for someone else? Why is something right or wrong in the first place? And if we shouldn't impose our morality, how come when it came to certain teachers' favorite causes (environmentalism, feminism, whatever), we weren't free to have a "value system" that disagreed with theirs?

The Church has a little different view of "value systems". The word *value* basically means "what something is worth". The difference between the way the Church sees "value" and the way the world sees it is that the world says we determine value by deciding what something is worth to us. If we like it, it has a lot of value. If we don't like it, it doesn't have value.

That might be a halfway decent approach, if you were talking about sofas or stereos or something. If you don't like a certain stereo, you won't pay much money for it. It doesn't have much value to you. If people are afraid that if they buy a fur coat someone will dump red paint on it the first time they wear it outside, then no one will buy fur coats any more, the cost will go down, and gas stations will start offering fur coats free with every fill-up. Their value will go down.

But that approach doesn't work when you get to the really important matters of life. Take you, for instance. What if someone doesn't like you? Your ex-girlfriend, for example. If she doesn't like you, does your value go down? Can she decide what you're worth? Do you want your entire value and dignity as a human being to be determined by a girl who has a grudge against you? Do you want other people's opinions to determine your value?

The Church, on the other hand, says that when God creates something, it has inherent worth, assigned by the Creator. That's the truth, the true value of something, and our role is to conform our understanding, our "value systems", to that truth.

For instance—human life. The Church tells us that every human life has infinite worth and infinite value, because every human being is made in the image and likeness of God. We aren't free, therefore, to say "Well, in my value system, human life isn't worth very much —especially unborn human life. So in my value system we can do anything we want to the unborn." That would be a "value system" based, not on the truth of the dignity of the human person, but on a lie. And basing our behavior on a lie leads to, you guessed it, moral confusion and personal insecurity. It's tough to feel secure when the value of everything, including yourself, can change at any time. And basing our be-havior on these sorts of lies also tends to lead to cruel atrocities against human life.

Or, for instance, sex. The world says we can determine our own "value systems" about sex. But we've discussed the fact that God says sex has a truth, a language, built right into it. It speaks the language of marriage, and we need to respect that truth. When we don't, and we base our behavior on a lie, we get hurt, because we're going against the way we're made.

Is it any surprise that we live in an age of "sad loneliness", of "moral confusion, personal insecurity, and easy manipulation"? An entire generation has been educated in "values clarification". Many of them are going around today thinking that they can all have these conflicting "value systems", never trying to ascertain the truth about how they're made or how they should live, and thinking that, as long as they "respect" each others' value systems, they'll all be fine.

But we can't just "respect" each others' conflicting value systems. They will collide constantly. If you value human life, and I don't, we're going to have a problem. "No country, not even the most powerful, can endure if it deprives its own children of this essential good." We can't have an ordered society if we don't base our laws, and our "value systems", on truth—the truth of the dignity of the human person, made in the image and likeness of God, and the rights and duties that flow from that dignity. We need constantly to challenge ourselves, and each other, to strive to understand this truth, and to apply it in our daily lives.

John Paul II says that these false teachers cause us to be "incapable of real love". Why is that?

Did you ever hear the phrase, "To know him is to love him"? Love, real love, is based on an accurate understanding of the truth of the beloved. If we don't know the truth, then our love is based on a lie. And love based on a lie can't be real love. So how can we love each other, or love God or His creation, if we don't really know the truth about what we're loving? Without an understanding of the truth of who we are, we're not just missing out on truth. We're missing out on love.

Next time someone asks you what's important in your value system, tell them that you think that the truth is pretty important. See how they respond. See if you can help nudge them out of this "values clarification" mindset and help them to see the real value of things.

You deserve the truth. Don't settle for cop-outs like "values clarification". Go straight to the divine "Source" and get the real story.

15

How Do I Know
When to Trust My Conscience?

*Why do the consciences of young people not rebel against this situa-
tion, especially against the moral evil which flows from personal
choices? . . . The normal thing would be for conscience to point out the
mortal danger to the individual and to humanity contained in the easy
acceptance of evil and sin. And yet, it is not always so. Is it because
conscience itself is losing the ability to distinguish good from evil?*

— *John Paul II, Denver, 1993*

So we know that, by following God, we can actually
determine the true value of the people and things around
us. But knowledge of those truths brings up another
question. How do we respond to those truths? Once we
know the value of another person or of the world around
us, how do we know if the way we're acting is in keeping
with their value? Questions of truth in value lead directly
to questions about truth in actions—questions of right
and wrong.

Why is it so easy for us to "miss the boat" sometimes?
Why is it so hard to figure out right and wrong? Why
do things that are wrong seem so right sometimes? And,

most important, where are our consciences when all of this is happening? If we're doing something wrong, won't our consciences bother us? Why do people not feel guilty when they're doing something the Church says is wrong?

These are the questions that John Paul II is asking. Why is it that so many of our consciences don't spot these problems? Why do they go on and on, largely unquestioned? Why do so many people seem so oblivious to sin? Where are our consciences when we need them?

His questions bring up questions we've all asked. What exactly *is* the conscience? How does it work? Is a person's conscience always correct—does it always reflect the truth? Are we supposed to follow our consciences no matter what?

I remember hearing people say, "Well, I know *you* think it's wrong ["it" meaning "sleeping with my boyfriend / having an abortion / shoplifting / dumping the Catholic Church to become a Moonie / whatever moral issue we happened to be disagreeing on that day"], but my conscience doesn't bother me, so I think it's okay." Sometimes that would make sense to me for a while. But then I'd see an ax murderer / serial killer on TV, and I'd hear him telling Geraldo Rivera that *he* had a clear conscience. So I knew something wasn't quite right.

John Paul II calls conscience "the voice of God, calling us to free ourselves from the grip of evil desires and sin". Wow! God is talking *directly* to us, giving us the truth, telling us how to live. It doesn't get any clearer than that.

So what about our friend the clear-conscienced serial killer? Is God telling him that it's really okay to be a serial killer, just as long as he feels good about himself? Somehow, looking at what we know about God, I'd tend to doubt that. God has some pretty clear ideas about right and wrong.

The trick, according to John Paul II, is that our conscience has to be "properly formed". He says that, in modern society, "the danger arises of wanting to manipulate conscience and its demands." We hear over and over that there is no objective reality, that there is no right and wrong, that we can determine our own value system, and that "truth" is whatever is good for you. And each time we hear that, it bends our conscience a little more. It's like a mirror that slowly warps, so that eventually it makes people look like midgets with enormous heads and no chests, and you have to sell it to the circus because no one else wants it. Modern society can distort our consciences so that we no longer hear the voice of God but just some kind of ridiculous distortion. The truth is no longer reflected.

Personally, I don't like that. I *like* the idea of having the voice of God talking to me through my conscience. He certainly makes more sense to me than most of the other voices I'm stuck with. So it's important to maintain the purity of the conscience. Jesus said, "The eye is the body's lamp. If your eyes are good, your body will be filled with light; if your eyes are bad, your body will be in darkness. And if your light is darkness, how deep will the darkness be!" (Mt 6:22–23).

How do we keep the "light" in our consciences? Believe it or not, John Paul II has the answer. (He makes my job really easy.) He says, "A rebirth of conscience must come from two sources: first, the effort to know objective truth with certainty, including the truth about God; and secondly, the light of faith in Jesus Christ, who alone has the words of life."

In other words, first you have to understand things, including God, the way they really are. You can say, "Well, *my* God is a god of greenness, and he doesn't care what I do as long as I always wear green, have a lot of money, and water my lawn." It may make you feel good, but it has nothing to do with the real God out there. You don't have your own god. There's only one.

Have you ever heard someone say, "Hey, man, that's your reality, not mine"? That has to be one of the stupidest statements in the entire English language.

Have you ever heard someone say, "Hey, man, that's your reality, not mine"? That has to be one of the stupidest statements in the entire English language. Just as you don't have your own "god", you don't have your own world, your own "reality", or your own truth. "Reality" is based on the word "real", meaning "actually existing". God created the reality around us, and He determined how it functions. To have a grip on reality means to understand that functioning, to understand cause and effect, and to live accordingly. And a part of that is understanding that certain actions cause damage to ourselves or others. Those actions are called sins. Just because you don't acknowledge something as a sin, or it's not a sin in your "reality", doesn't mean that it isn't a sin or that it won't do the damage that sin does. You need to learn about things as they are and to live in reality.

And, second, illuminate it all with a love for Jesus Christ and His Church. Remember, we can try to learn a whole lot, but we'll never know as much as He does, and we'll never love as much as He does. And He works today in and through His Church. So when the Church teaches something for two thousand years, that probably means He has something to do with it. The Church's teaching are "real". Listen to His Church, listen to Him, and talk to Him.

God made you with a conscience. He made you to hear His voice inside the deepest recesses of your heart—to point out problems, and to bug you when you're messing up. But if you don't take care of that little voice, you'll lose it. Be sure to feed your conscience a lot of good information. Fill it up with the truth. Don't expose it to just anything. Stay connected to God.

Because if you're hearing voices, you definitely want to make sure they're His.

16

Am I Supposed to Love *Myself*?

The truth about man—which the modern world finds so hard to understand—is that we are made in the image and likeness of God Himself, and precisely in this fact, apart from any other consideration, lies the inalienable dignity of every human being. . . . Look to Jesus Christ in order to see who you really are in the eyes of God!

— John Paul II, Manila, 1995

Only in Christ can men and women find answers to the ultimate questions that trouble them. Only in Christ can they fully understand their dignity as persons created and loved by God.

— John Paul II, Denver, 1993

So we understand the truth about God's creation. We understand how to fill our minds with that truth so that we can determine right from wrong. There's one more question.

Do you really understand the truth about yourself?

I don't mean just "Do you like yourself?" Ever since the seventies, the world seems to be full of people trying to like themselves better. Like Stewart Smalley on *Saturday Night Live*, they keep reminding themselves that "I'm good enough, I'm smart enough, and doggone it, people like me." The problem is, it never seems to work—for Stewart Smalley or anyone else.

We had self-esteem classes in high school that sounded pretty much the same. They were always telling us how special we were, but no one could ever come up with a particularly good reason *why* we were special. They had us list our good traits and talents and think about people who liked us, but it wasn't really enough to be convincing. What about the unpopular people? What about the ones who weren't sure of their talents? The basic result of those classes was that people who were doing things they shouldn't, like drugs, started saying, "Hey, man, this is the way I am, and I'm special. Don't bug me."

Am I saying that you're not special or that it's a bad thing to love yourself? No way. I think a lot of Christians don't really understand this. They think that Christian humility means that we should love God and look down on ourselves. But remember, Christ said, "Love your neighbor *as* yourself", not "Love your neighbor *instead* of yourself." We actually have a hard time really loving others until we've learned to love ourselves. Christ spent a lot of time telling us how much God loves us. Would it make sense for Him to love us that much if we shouldn't even love ourselves?

The question isn't whether or not we should love ourselves but rather *how* we should love ourselves and on what we should base that love. In trying to find the reason, John Paul II says, a lot of people in the modern world get confused.

Most people tend to base their self-worth on what they *do* or on their talents or abilities. They love themselves, and they think God loves them and others love them, because they're smart or good-looking or a good athlete. Their self-esteem grows when they're doing something they're good at or being reminded how beautiful they are, or whatever. That's fairly normal. But their self-esteem shrinks when they're not as beautiful (or haven't been *reminded* that they're beautiful), or when they have a bad performance, or when they mess up.

If we shouldn't base our worth on our talents or our looks, or anything about us, what *should* we base it on? John Paul II, as usual, has the answer. (Surprised?) He says, "Only in Christ can they fully understand their dignity as persons created and loved by God."

Think about this—even if you *were the only person in the world who needed saving, Christ would have gone through that hideous, awful, painful, horrifying death. For* you.

Are you special? You bet. How do you know? Because Jesus loved you enough to die on the Cross for you. Think about this—even if *you* were the only person in the world who needed saving, Christ would have gone through that hideous, awful, painful, horrifying death. For *you*. That's the truth about you.

God loves you a lot. More than you could ever possibly imagine. More than you could ever love yourself. And why? Does God love you because you're good-looking or because you're good at sports? No. God loved you before any of that. He loved you the first moment you were conceived in your mother's womb—created in His image and likeness. He created you in His image and likeness, and that's better than all the looks and talents in the world put together. It is *because* He loves you that He gave you life, with whatever talents and abilities you've been blessed.

Talents and abilities are not the reason God loves you. They are the "other considerations" John Paul II referred to in Manila. They're icing on the cake. He loved you first, before you had them. He'd love you even if you didn't have any other assets. He loves you when you're doing well. He loves you when you mess up. And He'll love you when your looks are gone, your talent has withered away, and your brain is addled. Anyone who wouldn't do the same doesn't really love you.

So what's our response? "Cool, God loves me no matter what. I can just be a lounge lizard all day—I don't have to prove myself." Not exactly. We have an obligation to *develop* those talents, not to make ourselves worthy of God's love, but as a *response* to it. When you give someone a beautiful gift, you're a little hurt when he shoves it in a closet and ignores it. Same with God. God gave us gifts and talents with the expectation that we'll use them to improve His world.

We also have an obligation not to sin. Why? Because when we sin, we're hurting each other, not to mention ourselves. We're hurting people whom God loves immensely. We're acting against something beautiful. It's because we're created in His image that we have a higher standard to which to conform. When we sin, we're not loving our neighbor *or* ourselves.

It's tough to avoid sin, because we've inherited this "original sin" problem. We seem to have a natural tendency to do things that *seem* like loving ourselves but are actually only selfish shortcuts that suffocate real love. That tendency to sin is something that we *shouldn't* love. We need to do all we can to starve it until it withers away, so we can replace it with the love of Christ—the real love that gets us where we want to go.

Loving yourself doesn't mean "I'm the most important person to me, so I'm going to take really good care of *me* and do nice things for me, and I don't care what happens to other people because I'm the really important one here." That's selfishness, and it's not "loving others as yourself". Selfishness is loving yourself instead of others. It's unattractive, sinful, and in the end it will make you a very lonely, bitter person. Real self-love means to understand your dignity and worth in the eyes of God, to engrave that understanding on the very deepest part of your psyche, and then to forget about yourself and concentrate on loving others. People who are secure in their dignity and their self-worth are free to forget about themselves. They don't have to waste their time and effort bolstering their egos and reminding themselves how special they are. They can spend their time loving others, reaching out to them, and living the fulfillment that comes from growing in love. Their security frees them to love.

It's normal to get a self-image boost when you do well or accomplish something. But don't forget why. Those accomplishments are *reminders* of God's love for us—reminders that He created you and gave you gifts and talents. But remember that He loves you even when things aren't going so well, even when you fail, and even when you don't love yourself.

God created you in His image and likeness. He blessed you with the incredible dignity of being called a child of

God. That worth and dignity can never, ever be taken away from you. You will carry it for life and carry it into eternity. Base your dignity and your self-worth on that.

God always loves you. Try to do the same.

17

What Are We Supposed to Be Doing While We're Here?

I come to Denver to listen to the young people gathered here, to experience their inexhaustible quest for life. Each successive World Youth Day has been a confirmation of young people's openness to the meaning of life as a gift received, a gift to which they are eager to respond by striving for a better world for themselves and their fellow human beings.

— John Paul II, Denver, 1993

Commit your youthful energies to the construction of the civilization of love.

— John Paul II, Buenos Aires, 1987

Young people know that their life has meaning to the extent that it becomes a free gift for others.

— John Paul II, Manila, 1995

The meaning of life.

When I was in high school, that was probably our favorite late-night discussion topic. This is not surprising. We were growing up and beginning to navigate the world on our own terms. It didn't take long to discover that it's a baffling world to steer through.

Sooner or later, everyone asks, "What's the point? Why am I here? What should I be working toward?" Of course, everyone has a different answer or philosophy of life. The existentialists say, "Well, you really can't keep life from being lousy, so just try to make the best of it." The hedonists say, "Live fast, die young, and leave a beautiful corpse." The beer commercials say, "Grab all the gusto you can get."

We all know people who live these philosophies. In fact, most of us probably know very few people who don't. Most of the time, they may seem like they're having fun. But in their more serious moments, they often encounter a profound emptiness. Suddenly the "good life" isn't enough. They haven't really found the meaning of life. They've just found a way to distract themselves so that they won't have to think about it. But that doesn't work forever.

We've already talked about how we find meaning and fulfillment in our lives through God, through living a relationship with Him and turning our lives over to Him. And we've talked about how life is a gift, given freely by God just because He loves us. And our job is to respond to that gift.

But where do we go from there? How do we adequately respond to such an amazing gift as our very selves, our very lives? How do we acknowledge this? How do we apply it to our lives?

John Paul II says that life has meaning to the extent that it becomes a free gift for others. In other words, we find meaning and happiness when we live, not for ourselves, but when we turn ourselves over to God and then let that love, His love, spill out through us into the surrounding world.

The Holy Father takes this statement from a line in the documents of Vatican II. (Bet you never thought you'd find anything interesting in there. See? Your Church is full of great surprises.) The line is this: Man can fully discover himself only through a sincere gift of himself.[1]

So that's how we find ourselves. I'm sure you've heard of other people going off to try to "find themselves". They quit their jobs, leave their families, and trek through the Himalayas, thinking they'll run across themselves somewhere. I have news for them. More people discover their true selves working in soup lines, or reaching out to a friend in need, than will ever find themselves wandering around the wilderness.

Have you ever had a day when you were depressed or sad? Stupid question, I know. But there's a second part. Have you ever then done something outside yourself— sending someone a card, comforting a crying child, visiting a nursing home—and then found that you felt better? This is what John Paul II is talking about. We feel better when we help each other.

God made us to go beyond ourselves. He made us to intertwine our lives with other peoples' lives, to exist beyond the little circle of ourselves. He made us to use the gifts we have to leave the world a little better place than we found it.

That "leaving the world a better place" applies in two ways. The obvious way, of course, is to love our friends, to be there for them, and to help each other out. But John Paul II says that God is asking more of us. That love is

[1] *Gaudium et Spes*, no. 24.

supposed to extend into the larger world, to "strive for a better world".

I believe that teenagers in particular are already aware of this on a very deep and profound level. I talk to a lot of teens every year, and I see an amazing idealism—a willingness to sacrifice to make the world a better place. I see youth camps going down to Mexico for outreach programs, sleeping in shacks on dirt floors so they can help those less fortunate than they are. I see teens cleaning up their communities. I see them starting petition drives.

I think the problem is that, over time, the cynicism of the adult world around them starts to seep in. So many adults don't believe that we can *really* change anything. It's a big world, and one little person can't do much. They believe that, in the end, everyone just needs to look out for himself. "You'll never eradicate poverty. Just stay home this summer and get a job."

That's one reason it's important to stay close to God and to pray regularly. He sees a "big picture" that we can't see. He shows us the way. He helps us figure out what to do next.

Sure, it's true that we'll never eradicate poverty. We'll never feed every homeless person or visit every old person. But think of the dent we'd make if each of us visited one or fed one. Or visited and fed a hundred.

The thing is, we're all the body of Christ. We're working together. Our efforts may seem small, but they can fit in with someone else's efforts somewhere else—maybe someone we don't even know. Maybe someone on the other side of the country or the other side of the world is doing something that will complement what you're doing right now. Together, your efforts can make a huge difference, especially when you're working in communion with Christ, the One who can make *anything* happen.

But how exactly do we start? How do we know where our talents and abilities fit in? How do we know what we're supposed to do with all of this?

The tricky part is, we can't know exactly. Only God can see the big picture. He knows what abilities He gave you and how your efforts could fit together to benefit the world. Maybe something you're doing seems insignificant to you. But God knows how it can grow, when combined with someone else's efforts.

That's one reason it's important to stay close to God and to pray regularly. He sees a "big picture" that we can't see. He shows us the way. He helps us figure out what to do next.

The Holy Father said that young people are "eager to respond" to this meaning of life. I think many people, especially young people, recognize the emptiness of the "live for now" culture, and they long for the fulfillment that comes from a life spent for others and for God. That's not hard to see. We see that longing in the enthusiastic response to the Holy Father's message at World Youth Day. We see it every week in the countless unselfish service projects of youth groups all over the country. We see it in the idealism of youth—an idealism constantly threatened by cynicism.

Don't give in to that cynicism. John Paul II certainly hasn't, and look what he's done. Plenty. Sure you can't do it all, but remember, there are a lot of you. And among all of you, there's a lot of love.

The Holy Father asked that you be accepted as "partners in the construction of a more humane, more just, more compassionate world".

I think you're up to the challenge.

18

God Wants *Me* to Spread the Gospel?

The Christian laity share in Christ's mission: the fathers and mothers of children, old people, young people, and children; simple people and those who are educated; people who till the soil, factory workers, engineers, technicians, doctors, nurses, and health care personnel.

— John Paul II, Manila, 1995

Be witnesses to the love of Christ!

— John Paul II, Buenos Aires, 1987

Proclaim His message of salvation to every person, every family, every people.

— John Paul II, Santiago de Compostela, 1989

Be messengers of the good news of salvation so that others will discover the meaning of life by encountering Jesus Christ.

— John Paul II, Czestochowa, 1991

Go into all the world and preach the Gospel to all creation (Mk 16:15).

— John Paul II, Denver, 1993

You are not being sent to proclaim some abstract truth. The gospel is not a theory or an ideology! The gospel is life!

— *John Paul II, Manila, 1995*

Do you get the feeling he's trying to tell us something?

Every World Youth Day, the Holy Father makes the same point. Preach the gospel. Spread the good news. Tell the world about your faith.

We just said that the meaning of life is to love. We tap into God and go out to help people—comforting the afflicted, feeding the hungry, and all of that. But there's something that people need even more than food or comfort. That something is God—the gospel. And a part of reaching out in love is bringing that gospel to them. John Paul II lets the world's youth know, in no uncertain terms, that God is calling them to bring that gospel to those around them. Evangelization—spreading the gospel, is his primary theme at every World Youth Day.

What does he mean when he tells us to preach the gospel? "Oh, well. Forget about being a doctor, or a lawyer, or a football player, or whatever. I guess I'm supposed to be some kind of preacher or missionary or something, like everybody else."

Wrong.

This is not the answer to the question "What do I want to be when I grow up?" It's the answer to the question "What should I be doing *while* I live my life?" Preaching the gospel isn't necessarily a job. It's just a part of life. *Everyone's* life.

Which part? Does it mean that lawyers should start interrogations by asking their defendants, "Have you accepted Jesus Christ?" Should doctors preach to their patients instead of curing them?

Wrong again.

To understand what Jesus really wants us to do, we have to understand what the gospel really is. The Holy Father says that the gospel isn't just some random theory. It's about life: *real* life. Gospel means "good news". You know, like hearing that a test was canceled, or getting a lot of cash for your birthday. Good news is something that makes you happy.

What's so great about what Jesus had to tell us? Basically, His good news is that God and man have been reunited and that eternal happiness is available to those who follow Him.

That's pretty big news, especially to today's culture, which is, in case you hadn't noticed, largely lonely and miserable. This is not surprising, without God in the picture. What is there really to look forward to? As the saying goes, "Life's a (expletive deleted) and then you die." Without hope of eternal life, that about sums it up.

But, as followers of Christ, we know that there can be something better. This life is only a "trial run". The best is yet to come, in heaven. We can be happy *forever!* I mean really happy, not just in a good mood part of the time. Not just having a good day but knowing that tomorrow everything could go rotten again. We can live all eternity being perfectly happy—totally fulfilled and knowing that we're never again going to be frustrated, lonely, or unfulfilled. I can't think of anything better, because there *is* nothing better. Eternal happiness is as good as it gets.

No wonder the Holy Father says that the gospel is life!

This is *great* news for the people around us. I'd like to tell *all* people about this. I think it could make a huge

difference in their outlook. It could make a huge difference in their lives. It could give them hope where right
now they have none. They can be happy forever.

What's the catch? Simple. All we have to do to gain that
eternal happiness is to strive to live life as Christ taught us.

"So that's the catch!" Yep, we have to live a certain way,
and we have to help others live it, too. What is that way?
Memorize a lot of rules and follow them? Look for
loopholes where we can? Study theology?

"Love one another as I have loved you." It all comes
back to love. Again. That's what Christ tells us to do. It's
the sum of all the commandments. It's how we find our
fulfillment. It's how we gain everlasting life. Of course,
we have to know the commandments and the teachings
of the Church, because sometimes God knows better
than we do what could hurt someone. But the heart of
the message is to love each other and God.

If we live *a certain way, it'll speak volumes
to those around us. What we do is far more
powerful than what we say.*

How do we "preach" this good news? Do we stand
up at student government meetings or football practice
and order everyone to love each other? Do we corner
our friends and read the Bible to them? Go for it if you
think you'll be effective, but I think there's a better
way.

"They will know we are Christians by our love." If we
live a certain way, it'll speak volumes to those around us.
What we do is far more powerful than what we say. If

people see a certain care and compassion in us, if they see a certain happiness and peace even when we're having problems, they'll know something is going on. They'll see something they want. And they'll ask about it.

When I first graduated from college, I worked for a computer company. A lot of the people who worked there were about my age, and I made a lot of really good friends.

When I was first getting to know people there, they sometimes made conversation by asking, "What did you do last night?" More often than not, my answer would be "I went to Mass." I wasn't bragging, I wasn't trying to make a point, I was just answering the question. I usually went to daily Mass in the evenings.

It was almost funny to see the looks on their faces.

The "former Catholics" would be racking their brains trying to figure out if it had been some obscure holy day they had forgotten about. The rest would either retreat in stunned silence or manage to sputter out "Church? Why? Yesterday was *Wednesday*."

As time went on, I could see them kind of watching me. They weren't hostile, just curious. It was like the way sociologists would observe a primitive tribe. They had discovered a rare creature—a modern woman who attends daily Mass and *isn't even a nun!*

Eventually, they figured out that, despite the fact that I went to daily Mass, I really wasn't so bad as a person. I liked parties. I cracked occasional jokes. I wasn't a miserable, self-righteous prig. I was fairly normal.

Once they trusted me, they suddenly wanted to know more. The questions started. "So why would someone our age be into religion, anyway? What's the deal with this God thing? What about Jesus? Did He really come to earth? What about sex? What's the big deal about being Catholic?"

It was amazing. I spent a *lot* of time, probably a lot more than I should have, in hallway discussions, in phone discussions, and on e-mail, answering theological questions. It kept me on my toes, that's for sure. These were smart, well-educated people. They had some good questions—hard questions. I had to read up; I had to do research. I had to know my stuff.

That experience made me realize a couple of things. First, that I am, and we all are, living examples of Christianity. That gives us a certain responsibility. We're Christ's presence in the visible world. We've got to act like it. When people see us being cruel or not respecting our sexuality, it's not just like when the rest of the world does those things. It's "those hypocritical Christians". We can give Christianity a bad name. More important, we can keep them from seeing that inner radiance, that peace that would draw *them* to Christ. Our actions, good or bad, determine whether others will find Christ. That's a big responsibility.

I also realized that the most effective evangelization is to live the best life I can and not try to hide it. I don't have to go out trumpeting it or put it on display. Living well, or striving to live well, becomes apparent to others. And living well can draw others to Him. It's the best way to "preach".

I also realized that I'd darned well better know as many answers as I could. People can be smart, and they can ask really good questions. If I'm Christ's representative at that given point in time, I'd better be able to do a good job. The same goes for everyone. If we're going to preach by example, we'd better be able to explain our actions.

It all boils down to this—if we love Christ, and love those around us, we have to act like it. And we have to understand *why*, so that when others ask us about our faith, we can give them the answers.

That's preaching the gospel. It's a lot easier than becoming a televangelist and probably a lot more effective.

19

But How Can I Get Up the Guts to Talk to My Friends about This Christianity Stuff?

But we human beings have this treasure in earthen vessels (2 Cor 4:7). That is why we are often afraid of the demands of the Redeemer's love. . . . Yet the fact that we carry this treasure in earthen vessels makes it clear that its surpassing power comes from God and not us. Whenever young men and women allow the grace of Christ to work in them and produce new life, the extraordinary power of divine love is released into their lives and into the life of the community. It transforms attitudes and behavior and inevitably attracts others to follow the same adventurous path. This power comes from God and not us.

— *John Paul II, Denver, 1993*

How does Jesus send you? He promises neither sword, nor money, nor power, nor any of the things which the means of social communications make attractive to people today. He gives you instead grace and truth.

— *John Paul II, Manila, 1995*

You know the feeling. You're standing around in a group of people, and some of them are talking down the

Church. Or they're talking about sleeping with someone. Or they're talking about being "pro-choice", and how pro-lifers are stupid.

You know you should speak up. You know the truth, and you know that these people are misleading others, not to mention the fact that they're misled themselves. But you think, "Naah. It wouldn't do any good anyway. I'm just one person, and her mind is made up. Besides, if I say something now, it'd just alienate her, so I couldn't do any good later."

Translation: "To speak up might jeopardize my popularity, or my friendships, or my status."

The "treasure" we hold is God's love and the graces He won for us on the Cross. The "earthen vessel" is our bodies—with our emotions, feelings, and ego. And those "vessels" are afraid. They're afraid of being laughed at. They're afraid of not being popular. They're afraid of being different or alone.

Our vessels are wimps.

Too bad, too, because the treasure we have is pretty awesome. It's the ultimate love. It's everlasting life. It's eternal happiness. It's something we want, not just for ourselves, but for everyone around us as well—especially the people we love, like our friends.

What do we do? It *does* seem pretty unrealistic to expect that we could change their minds. They have been exposed to messages contrary to Christianity all of their lives. They've been seeing all of those things that "the means of social communications make attractive"— things like promiscuous sex, disposable marriages, instant gratification, and basic selfishness. Those messages are easier—they allow them to go on down the "wide road".

How are we supposed to convince them to "take up

their cross" for a distant reward when it can be really hard in the short run? How are we supposed to make Christianity as attractive as MTV? Why should we jeopardize our friendships, our status, and our popularity when we're probably going to fail anyway? It'd be one thing if it worked. But for nothing?

Well, there's one power we forgot to take into account. God's. Of course we couldn't possibly convince anyone by ourselves. We're earthen vessels. We're weak and chicken. We're dealing with original sin.

But that treasure in us is stronger than we know. We're not the ones doing the convincing. God is.

The Apostles Were Wimps, Too

Have you ever read the story of Pentecost in the Acts of the Apostles? You may relate to it.

Jesus was gone. He had ascended into heaven. He had left the apostles with a mandate, "Go into all the world and preach the gospel to the whole of creation" (Mk 16:15).

They knew what they had to do. Only there was one little catch. They could be killed just preaching in their own *neighborhood*. They wouldn't be risking just their popularity or their friendships or their status. They would be risking their lives. Jesus had already been killed, and no one was particularly interested in His followers stirring up any trouble. There were plenty of crosses around Jerusalem, and the Romans weren't afraid to use them.

So the apostles were "hanging out". In a room. With the door locked. They were hiding. "Stalling" would probably be a good description. They were probably figuring they'd start spreading the good news a little later.

"When things have settled down a little bit." "When the Romans forget what we look like." "When we're a lot older and don't mind dying so much."

They were scared.

But then something strange happened. The wind started blowing—inside the house. The apostles had spent a lot of time with Jesus, and they'd seen a lot of weird things happen. They knew when He was up to something. This was definitely one of those times.

Then "there appeared to them tongues as of fire, distributed and resting on each one of them. And they were all filled with the Holy Spirit, and began to speak in other tongues" (Acts 2:3–4).

Suddenly these wimpy, scared guys were energized. They unlocked the doors and went outside. Then they started preaching. Not only were they preaching, but they were speaking languages they didn't even know. Different people were hearing the same words in different languages. People weren't used to the apostles being so powerful. They actually figured that the apostles must be drunk (Acts 2:13).

Suddenly these wimpy, scared guys were energized. They unlocked the doors and went outside. Then they started preaching. Not only were they preaching, but they were speaking languages they didn't even know.

But they weren't. They were given grace and truth. They were "filled with the Holy Spirit". And that Spirit made them very effective evangelists. He gave them words that they couldn't have come up with on their own. Most important, He convinced people of the truth of the gospel. These wimpy apostles, with no money, no power, and no network television, converted over three thousand people that day (Acts 2:41).

Pretty good for a bunch of wimps.

The story of Pentecost is the story of the first confirmation class. What happened to them happens to us in that little ceremony where the bishop anoints our heads with oil and then slaps us. It isn't quite as jarring as tongues of fire, but it's the same concept.

God calls us all to evangelization—to spreading the good news of His Kingdom throughout the earth. But God never gives us an assignment without also giving us the power to carry it out. That's what confirmation is about—it's about accepting Christ as adult Christians and accepting our mission as Christians to improve the world, love our fellow man, and preach the gospel.

In order to do that, we're going to need a lot of help—a lot of grace. And that's what we receive in confirmation. We receive the Holy Spirit in a special way, to give us the power and the strength to go out into an often hostile world, just as the apostles did.

The Holy Spirit—an "Inside Job"

So what exactly is this "Holy Spirit"? Quite simply, He's God. The Holy Spirit is the third Person of the Trinity. His role is to act in us, to help us to be the best people we can, and to make us effective at doing God's work on earth. He's the one who enabled the apostles to convert three thousand people in one day when they had been too scared to go outside. And He's the one who enables us to "spread the good news" to our friends. He's the one we receive in a special way in the sacrament of confirmation.

The beautiful thing about the Holy Spirit is that He's an "inside job".

First of all, He's an inside job on us as we evangelize. He doesn't leave us on our own, but He gives us the right words. Just as He helped the apostles to speak in languages they'd never spoken before, He can help us explain things in a "language" our friends will understand. We don't necessarily know what these other people need to hear or how to be most convincing to them. But He does, and He can speak through us, helping us to understand what they need and to say it articulately.

Second, He's an inside job on the people we're talking to. We can only say the words, but He can take these words to their hearts and give them the grace to understand and to accept His words and His truth. Sure, it'd be a miracle to influence them. But miracles are God's specialty.

This insight is particularly inspiring to me. As many of you know, I go around the country talking about chastity—helping teenagers understand why they should wait to have sex until they're married. Talk about scary! God's plan for sex can be difficult to discuss with people, especially people who have bought into the "means of social communication". Your average Madonna video is not really about respect for sexuality. So it can be incredibly tough just to tell a couple of your friends about chastity. Imagine telling thousands of teenagers at a time.

I was scared the first time I gave a talk. But I did it anyway, because I knew God wanted me to, and I knew that if it worked, it would be only because He was helping me. And He did! I was speaking to a junior high class, and their teachers told me that they *never* sat still for more than twenty minutes. But they listened and asked questions for over an hour and a half. They even voluntarily skipped their recess so they could hear more. They wanted to skip lunch, but their teacher wouldn't let them. Afterward several came up to thank me and said that they had learned a lot about how to treat their gift of sexuality.

Since then I've spoken to hundreds of thousands of teenagers. I've had a lot of enthusiastic responses and a lot of standing ovations. Imagine, teenagers giving standing ovations for chastity! But I know it's not me generating all of that enthusiasm. It's the Holy Spirit. He's giving me the words they need to hear, and He's taking those words to the deepest parts of their hearts. And He does a really good job—much better than I could ever do.

Alone, there's no way I could go up against the attitudes in society that contradict the Church's message. Alone, there's no way I could even understand His plan for sexuality, much less explain it. But I'm not alone. It's His work, His words, and His power that keep me going. My part is to learn all I can, pray a lot, and keep showing up. And now I'm never scared—because I know it's not me. It's Him and His work. And through Him, that work has been more successful than I ever dreamed it could be.

The same goes for you. When you hear God calling you to do something you don't want to, like speaking up for Him, don't let your "vessel" get the best of you. Turn it over to Him. Trust Him to help you out. Ask Him to send His Spirit.

Doing Your Part

Does all of this mean that you can just blurt out any old thing, no matter how reactionary you sound, and trust the Holy Spirit to clean it up for you? No. God takes our best work and makes it bear fruit. But we have to give Him the best our "vessels" can do. We need to understand Him and put a lot of good material into our brains so that He has a lot to choose from when giving us the right words. He won't usually just pour knowledge into your head. But He will organize what you've put there and draw it together into new insights that will dazzle you and will touch the hearts of those around you. So your part is really to work to learn all you can about Him. Reading this book is a good start. But don't stop here. Go to a Catholic bookstore. Read other books. Read the *Catechism of the Catholic Church*. Read *the* book—the Bible. It's not really that hard, you know. Just buy one of those little daily missals, and every day read the readings for the Mass that day. Or better yet, go to Mass and hear them for yourself. The important thing is to put a lot of material into your brain for the Holy Spirit to work with.

Above all, remember that God is love. We need to be constantly aware of that and to strive to present Him that way. And He, through His love and His Spirit, is the one to help us do that.

God's grace, through the Holy Spirit, "transforms attitudes and behaviors, and inevitably attracts others to follow the same adventurous path". That's a pretty cool thing to do—to bring others along with you on the path to salvation. You're giving them a gift they'll never lose— eternal happiness with God in heaven. If you help them get there, they'll be pretty grateful. They'll spend eternity thanking you.

There are a lot of ways to increase the action of the Holy Spirit in our lives. Confirmation is one. If you haven't been confirmed, now is the time to sign up for a class. If you have been confirmed, you should regularly renew the commitment you made to God in your confirmation.

Ask God to send you His Spirit. Pray constantly—for help, guidance, and inspiration. Then, yield yourself to His action, get up your guts, do His work, and hang on for the ride of your life. You're not just a vessel anymore.

You're turbocharged.

20

Could It Be, Hmm . . . , Satan?

This marvelous world—so loved by the Father that He sent His only Son for its salvation—is the theater of a never-ending battle being waged for our dignity and identity as free, spiritual beings.

— *John Paul II, Denver, 1993*

So we're "spreading the gospel". We're evangelizing the world. We're telling everybody about the good news about how God loves us, Christ died for us, and we can live happily ever after if we follow Him. And we've got the Holy Spirit to make sure we say it right.

What could go wrong?

A lot. The problem is that we have opposition. Big opposition. As John Paul II says, there's a battle being waged over us—a battle "for our dignity and identity as free, spiritual beings".

The concept of "battle" implies the existence of combatants on opposing sides. Who are they? Well, we've seen the lineup for our side. We're the ones out in the battlefield, spreading the gospel. We're operating under the brilliant leadership of our three-Person Commander in Chief, God. God the Father is directing the action. Christ actually came down into the trenches to help us out. And the Holy Spirit acts in and through all of us, fortifying us for battle.

Quite an impressive cast of characters. Who's lined up on the other side?

Well, their leader is someone everyone seems to have forgotten about. (Well, everyone except the Church Lady on *Saturday Night Live*.) They're led by the Prince of Darkness, the Father of Lies, the Evil One. Their leader is Satan—the devil.

It's not particularly popular to believe in Satan these days. Most people, when they think of the devil, think of a little horned guy in red tights, and they can't believe anyone could take him seriously. They laugh it all off, and they figure they don't need to worry about him.

I figure we *do* need to worry about him. I have it on pretty good authority that we should. Christ said so Himself—constantly. Read the New Testament some-time. Christ was always warning us about the Evil One and telling us to remain strong and vigilant so that we wouldn't be susceptible to his traps and temptations. The whole reason Christ came was to conquer Satan and to release the grip he had on the world.

Satan is not a man, and he's not a god. He's an angel—an angel gone *really* bad. What happened was something like this. When God created the angels, He created them, as He created us, with free will. They could choose to accept or reject Him. It's hard to imagine an angel reject-ing God. After all, they're right there with Him. They can see Him. They know how great He is. But, for some reason, Satan and his crew rejected God anyway. They refused to worship God. They wanted to be number one, and God was getting in the way.

Well, heaven's an awfully big place, but there's no room

there for anyone who won't worship God. They just don't fit in. Since these guys weren't going to play by the rules, they were cordially invited to leave. They were thrown out.

Where did they go? They went to the only place where they would be comfortable. Those who reject God are very uncomfortable in His presence. God is all goodness and love, and so to reject God is to reject goodness and love. Once you've rejected that love, you don't want to be around it. After rejecting God, they needed to be far away from Him. So Satan and his followers were sent to the only place where God is not present.

That place, of course, is hell.

Satan tries to make sin look really appealing to us. He tells us sin will make us better, stronger, happier people.

So what's he doing down there today? Feeling sorry for himself for missing out on heaven? No way. He's so far from God he can't even comprehend that. Besides, he's too busy. He's trying to get *us* down there to join him. I guess misery loves company.

How does he operate? He works on our free will. We have the ability to accept or reject God, just as he did. God wants us to accept. Satan wants us to reject. And he tries to influence us to reject. He tries to make sin look really appealing to us. He tells us sin will make us better, stronger, happier people. He whispers to us, just as he whispered to Adam and Eve, "You shall be like gods."

Being an angel, Satan is a whole lot more powerful than humans are. He's faster and smarter. He can go from place to place instantly. He can influence us inside our brains. He can distort our attitudes and the circumstances of our lives.

Satan is *not*, however, as powerful as God. He's not some kind of equal "anti-God" that God is always having to do hand-to-hand battle with, hoping to win so that He can work His plan without interference. God created Satan, and He could crush him in a heartbeat.

A teacher of mine once told me that Satan is like a football coach. He watches the films of our lives like a coach watching the films of last week's game. And then he plans his strategy. Where are you weak? Where are there openings he can get into? When is your guard down?

Once he's found those openings, he uses them relentlessly. Are you lonely? He'll tempt you with sex or with a relationship with someone he knows is dangerous to you spiritually. Depressed? He'll tempt you with booze or drugs. Happy? He'll convince you it was all your doing, and you don't need God in your life at all.

How do we overcome this enemy? First of all, we need to know that God has already overcome him. We know how the war ends, and we know that God wins. But in the middle, we could be casualties if we're not careful.

We avoid being casualties by putting on the "armor of Christ". We need to stay very, very close to Him, and we need His grace and His Holy Spirit constantly active in our lives. That Spirit gives us the wisdom to see Satan and his temptations for what they really are—counterfeits taking us away from the love of God. And He gives us the strength to resist him.

There is an excellent book by C. S. Lewis on the subject of Satan. It's called *The Screwtape Letters*. It's written as correspondence between a young devil and his uncle, a senior devil, instructing the younger devil in the art of temptation. It's easy to read, very humorous in parts, and it gives amazing insights into the myriad of ways that Satan can wedge his way into our daily experiences and lead us down the wrong path. It's one of the best books I've ever read, and I highly recommend it.

If we're going to follow God, and if we want to lead others to Him, we need to take Satan very seriously. We shouldn't get lazy and figure we'll be fine on our own, because we won't. He's a lot smarter than we are, and he knows exactly where we're weak. We'd be really stupid to try to resist him on our own. We need to be constantly on our guard, and we need to keep close to God. We do have an enemy, and he's plenty smart. We can't win this one without having God on our team.

21

Is the Church Really against Contraception?

The Church calls married couples to responsible parenthood by acting as "ministers"—not as "arbiters"—of God's saving plan.

— John Paul II, Denver, 1993

As we're out evangelizing our way through our everyday lives, we're going to run up against some questions about God and about the Catholic Church. Some of those questions are tougher than others, but we need to be able to answer as many of them as possible.

One of the first questions most people have about Catholicism is "Why isn't birth control allowed for Catholics?" It seems like everyone, from the media to the ladies' bridge group, loves to talk about the Catholic Church and contraception.

Now that particular teaching is not exactly on the "Top Ten Popular Teachings List" for Catholics. Whenever pollsters want to show us how rebellious Catholics are, they always ask about this teaching, figuring it's an easy story. A lot of Catholics don't follow it.

But what amazes me is how few Catholics *understand* this teaching. In fact, I wonder how many of *you* understand it. Being a member of the media myself, I've devised a little quiz to test your knowledge. Be careful, it's tricky.

CONTRACEPTION QUIZ

The Church teaches that artificial birth control is wrong because:

A. The Pope wants to ruin our sex lives.
B. The Church wants everyone to have 14 children so that Catholics can take over the world.
C. The oppressive male patriarchy is conspiring against women.
D. None of the above.

If you said "D", you were right. But just because you know what the teaching is not doesn't mean you know what it *is*. Read on.

As we said in the chapter on marriage, the Church's view of sex is *not* negative, as many people think, but is actually amazingly positive—more positive than any of the currently popular philosophies. The Church doesn't say that sex is dirty, she says that sex is *holy*. That holiness is based on two facts. First, as we've said, sex is "body language". Sex doesn't just say "I like you", or even "I love you." It says, "I give myself to you forever, and I dedicate my life to what's best for you."

Second, sex is holy because God chose it, *that* act of permanent, self-giving love, to perform His most creative act. Through sex, He creates a new individual with an eternal soul—an individual who's never existed before and whom He loves madly. That makes sex awfully important to Him.

So sex is God's in a unique way. In sexual union, God is *there*, prepared to create a new life. Even when infertile couples perform that act of His out of love for Him and each other, He is there. With God, love is always fruitful. It always goes beyond itself. It always leads to new, good things.

But what happens when we use artificial birth control? We're *changing* sex, rerouting God's act to suit *our* purposes. We're taking an act where He is present, and we're blocking Him out. We're dis-inviting Him. We're saying, "My way or the highway, God." We're being arbiters, not ministers.

What's an Arbiter?

Speaking of which, what was the Pope talking about with this "arbiter" and "minister" stuff, anyway?

To be "ministers" of God's plan means to work within it—to cooperate with Him to make His plan happen. To be an "arbiter", on the other hand, means to take control, to say "I don't care about your plan; this is *my* plan."

It's an amazing privilege to cooperate with God, especially in something as important to Him as creating new human life. After all, He could have created a system where He had more direct control—dropping babies out of the sky or delivering them via UPS. But he chose to let us help, working through our act of love.

With this privilege comes tremendous responsibility. The Pope keeps talking about God's "plan". What is this plan? His plan of salvation. Who's He saving? He's saving His people. Who are His people? The ones He creates, working through us. Starting to get the picture?

I believe He has people in mind before they're even conceived. I believe He had me in mind before I was conceived, and I believe he knew about you, and loved you, before you were conceived. But He needed the openness and cooperation of our parents to make us happen. They were ministers of His plan in giving us life. They had to make a lot of sacrifices to do it, from the inconvenience of pregnancy to the horror of four-year college tuition. But their openness paid off in a big way—you!

Conceived outside of Marriage—
Not Part of the Plan?

What if you weren't conceived as a result of the married love of a husband and a wife? What if you were conceived as a result of two teenagers who made a mistake on prom night? What if you were conceived as a result of rape? What if you were adopted and have no idea what the circumstances of your conception were? What does all of this "God's plan" stuff say about you? Does it include you?

I think there is sometimes a temptation for people to wonder. They think that if God has a plan, but their existence doesn't fall into line with that plan, then they must be some kind of cosmic "accident", someone God didn't really plan on, and now He's not too sure what to do about it. Or they figure He might not love them as much as He loves others.

There's something we have to get straight from the outset. God loves every single human being who ever existed, from the very first moment of that person's existence. Remember, your parents didn't create you. God did. Your parents performed the act that set the biological part of your creation in motion, but God created you. He created your soul, as well as every fiber of your physical being. And He loves—with the same overwhelming, infinite love—every single person He has created, without exception. There's no one He loves more, and no one He loves less. He loves each and every one of us with the same awesome, overwhelming love. So no matter who else loves you or doesn't, even if *no one* else loves you, He does. He wants you to exist, and He has a plan for you. Be sure of that.

Why Did It Happen This Way?

So why did God allow you, whom He loves so much, to be born outside the plan? Well, this one is probably bigger than our little minds can grasp. We know that He wants new life in families for a reason—because we should have two parents if possible. It is really nice to have two parents who love each other, so that we can learn about love from watching them. And He entrusted us, people who are prone to original sin, with this system, knowing that sometimes people would use it outside of that plan.

So no matter who else loves you or doesn't, even if no one *else loves you, He does. He wants you to exist, and He has a plan for you. Be sure of that.*

We know that God won't act as some kind of "divine birth control", keeping unmarried people from getting pregnant. But we also know that His plan accounts for people's actions and mistakes. After all, He knows about everything in advance. It's not as if He's "surprised" when someone gets pregnant. He knew you were coming, and He wanted you to.

There's an old saying: "God writes straight with crooked lines." That means that, no matter what circumstances, or even broken messes, we're born into or happen to us later, God loves us madly. And He'll take whatever circumstances we're given and work with them.

Were you adopted? God brought you together with a family that wanted you desperately and that loves you. Is your mom a single mother? God is still your father, regardless of where your biological father is. He gives your mom extra graces, I'm sure, to live her responsibilities. And I'll bet that if you asked Him and then looked around, there'd be some men in your life who could act as "father figures" for you.

Most important, do you know someone in this situation right now? If someone is pregnant out of wedlock, for whatever reason, it's important to remember that, no matter what, there is a life growing inside of her—a life created by God in His image and likeness and a part of His plan. Make sure she knows that.

God is not a random kind of God. He created the world, and He holds it in existence at every moment. He knows what He is doing. But He doesn't leave us out. He created the world for us, and He invites us to participate in bringing the next generation of His people into existence. He invites us to be ministers of His plan. Even knowing that we'll sometimes be imperfect ministers, that we may mess up His timing, He still allows us to join in His creative work. It's a tremendous privilege.

So Do Catholics Just Have to "Crank Out Babies"?

Let's get back to contraception. We talked about why the Church doesn't approve of it. But does this mean that all Catholic families have to have as many kids as biologically possible?

Sometimes families really can't afford another child. Sometimes pregnancy would threaten a woman's health. Sometimes moms are just exhausted from having lots of little kids around and need a break from having more. Is the Church so insensitive that she has no compassion for these people?

There's no law that says that Catholics need to have as many children as is biologically possible. Children are a gift. They're created in the image of God, with immortal souls. But children are also a responsibility, for the same reasons. The idea isn't to "breed" as many as possible and then leave them to fend for themselves. We're called to *form* them, to help them grow into adults who know and love God and who develop and use their talents in His service. That's a big job. And different people have different capacities. Some couples have the strength and resources to raise fourteen children well. Others may not.

What should a couple do if they feel they should postpone another pregnancy? Do they need to go against the rules and change God's system by artificially contracepting?

No. God knew that there would be this need—that women would need time between the birth of each baby, and that sometimes couples would need to postpone pregnancy. So He made women's bodies with naturally fertile times and naturally infertile times. And He gave us ways of figuring out which is which. By abstaining from intercourse during the fertile time, a married couple can avoid pregnancy. This is called Natural Family Planning, or NFP.

NFP—Working with God

Now, before we go any farther, I want to talk about what NFP *isn't*. NFP is not, as some people say, the "Rhythm" method. Rhythm is a system, used widely by Catholics in the 1960s and earlier, where a woman keeps track of how long her menstrual cycles last and then uses that information to guess how long they'll last in the future and when she'll be fertile. It's not very effective. But it is, interestingly enough, about as effective as the best artificial methods that were available at the same time, like the condom. NFP, a more advanced method, arrived at about the same time that the Pill was introduced. Natural methods tend to keep pace with artificial methods in effectiveness.

Rhythm is guesswork. NFP isn't. A woman's body gives off definite signs when she is fertile. Her temperature rises. Her cervical mucus changes in appearance and consistency. (Gross? Maybe, but pretty interesting, too.) By monitoring these signs, a woman isn't guessing when she's fertile. She knows. Her body is telling her. When a couple watches those signs and abstains during the fertile time, NFP is extremely effective.

Can NFP Be Abused?

One hot topic of debate among Catholics is the question of when it's okay to use NFP. Can we just say, "Cool, now we can buy that BMW and that yacht. We'll just use NFP so we don't have any of those expensive kids running around"? Hardly. Remember how we talked about being "ministers" and not "arbiters" of God's plan? What's more important to have—a yacht that's eventually going to get barnacles and sink or a child with an immortal soul? What happens if a couple puts selfish greed ahead of openness to life? As Ricky Ricardo on *I Love Lucy* would say, they're going to have some 'splaining to do. To God. New life is a gift, and He expects us to be generous in bringing it into the world.

There's a big difference between avoiding pregnancy because it would threaten a mother's health or unreasonably stretch a family's time and resources, and postponing for selfish reasons like a yacht. Sometimes it's a fine line, and a couple needs to make decisions like this carefully and prayerfully. It's not up to us to look at them and judge, because we can't fully know their circumstances. But God does, and He'll guide them if they ask. He knows His plan—they're just the "ministers".

But Isn't NFP Just Catholic Birth Control?

Sometimes there are good reasons for a couple to postpone pregnancy, reasons like health, financial duress, or some other factor that would legitimately hinder their ability to raise and form the children they currently have. If they really need to postpone having children, what's the difference between NFP and other artificial methods? Isn't NFP just Catholic birth control?

To understand this, we have to go back a little bit. Remember when we talked about how sacred sex is— how God's favorite act is bringing new life into the world, and how He chose sex as the act He would work through to do that? God is present in sex—concretely there, prepared to perform His most creative act. But when we contracept, we "block God out". We dis-invite Him, and tell Him we're changing sex to suit our purposes. Even if our motives are good, blocking God out is not a good way to carry them out.

Compare that to NFP. God made the infertile time, too. He made it because He knew parents couldn't handle having a baby every time they engaged in sexual inter-course. They'd never be able to make houses big enough. He's present in the infertile time—He created it. To use that time isn't blocking Him out or taking over His plan. It's working within His plan.

Look at it another way. Remember how we talked about how sex speaks a language? Sex says, "I take all of you. Forever. Just the way you are." But what does contraceptive sex say? It says, "I take most of you, but your fertility is a little bit of a problem to me. In order to be acceptable to me, you need to change it. Get rid of it."

NFP, on the other hand, recognizes and accepts the woman as she is and acts accordingly. A woman's fertility is a part of her, a part of who she is at that time. If it isn't best for her to get pregnant, a loving husband understands and respects that. He can put her best interest above his desires and abstain when she's fertile. That's a way to accept her.

My friend Janet Smith gives a lot of talks on this, and she explains it this way. She says that contraceptive sex "says" something different from noncontraceptive sex. Contraceptive sex doesn't say much. It can say, "I find your body attractive" or "I want to have sex with you." But noncontraceptive sex says, "I take all of you. I'm permanently committed to you. This act could result in a baby, and if it does it's okay because we're committed for life."

Janet cites a study on unmarried women who have abortions.[1] It reported that many of them, even though they knew about contraception, chose not to use it. And one of the main reasons they gave was that non-contraceptive sex seemed to "prove" something more. They wanted to feel that they had a deeper level of commitment than contraceptive sex would indicate. Of course it doesn't work, but they instinctively know the difference.

Most contraceptives are pretty unpleasant. Condoms and foams are messy and ineffective. The Pill, Depo-Provera, and Norplant are powerful hormones that work on your *brain*, giving you hormonal overload (and side effects like nausea, metabolic changes, skin changes, blood clotting, and stroke risks). Women put up with this every day of the month, just to deal with a few days of fertility.

Worse than that, the Pill, Norplant, Depo-Provera, and the IUD often act by allowing conception to happen and then changing the lining of the uterus so that the baby, prevented from implanting, dies before the mother even knows she is pregnant. That's not contraception; it's abortion, and the implications are staggering. Millions and millions of women use these devices every month. Many of them, some estimate as high as 50 percent, are actually conceiving a child, a child known and loved by God, and that child is dying before it has a chance to see the light of day. And the mother doesn't even know it.

We can't be randomly creating new life and destroying

[1] Kristin Luker, *Taking Chances: Abortion and the Decision Not to Contracept* (Berkeley, 1975).

it. That isn't being "ministers" of God's plan. And it isn't a particularly effective way to "manage" women's fertility.

If you're a woman, what's going to make you feel loved? What kind of man do you want to marry? Someone who would say, "You have to put up with this mess/inconvenience/powerful drug/possible abortion because I want you to be sexually available to me"? Or a man who would say, "I love you, and if we decide to postpone pregnancy, I'll accept you and your body the way you are, and find other ways to express my love for you on your fertile days"?

I'll take bachelor number two.

22

Abortion: How Can I Impose My Morality on Anyone Else?

To follow Christ is to protect human life in all its stages.

— *John Paul II, Santiago de Compostela, 1989*

In her vigorous concern for human rights and justice, the Catholic Church is unambiguously committed to protecting and cherishing every human life, especially the unborn.

— *John Paul II, Denver, 1993*

Abortion.

It's a subject we *really* don't want to evangelize about. We know how controversial abortion is. We see fights about it all the time—on TV, in our schools, and often in our own homes.

Many times we just want to stay out of it. We want to get along with our friends. We don't want to argue. Life is too complicated anyway, without having to bring global issues into our friendships. So we say, "Sure I'm a Catholic. Sure I'm against abortion. I mean, I wouldn't have one personally. But that's my morality. I can't impose it on someone else. If she wants to have an abortion, it's her business."

It's a lot more comfortable that way, isn't it? I mean, everybody's happy. You're against it, just the way a good Catholic should be. But you leave room for other people's "values". Who can argue with that?

I can. And I will.

To test yourself, take the above statement, and replace the word "abortion" with something else you're opposed to. Like "I'm against rape. I mean, I wouldn't do it. But I can't impose my morality on others. If they want to rape, it's their business." Or "I'm opposed to racism, but if you want to be a racist. . . ."

Now, if we were talking about "values" like what kind of perfume you use or whether you believe in "great taste" or "less filling", then maybe there's room to "respect other people's values". But that doesn't work in rape or racism. Why? Because in rape or racism, it goes beyond the person to someone else. There's a victim.

If that's "just" a thimbleful of tissue, then everyone else is "just" a tubful of tissue.

And there's a victim in abortion. It's easy to forget about this victim, because you can't see her (or him). It's easy to want to believe that this is just a "thimbleful of tissue" that's disposed of in an abortion. But, as my brother once said, if that's "just" a thimbleful of tissue, then everyone else is "just" a tubful of tissue. It's not how much tissue there is, but *what* the tissue is that counts.

That "thimbleful of tissue", by the earliest abortion, is a person with a heartbeat, brain waves, fingers, and toes. She sucks her thumb, wakes and sleeps, and, according to increasing evidence, feels pain. If you've ever seen the video *The Silent Scream*, you know what I mean. It shows an ultrasound of an actual abortion. You can *see* the baby trying to dodge the abortionist's instruments. You see the heart rate suddenly double in fear. You see her being dismembered. If you're "personally opposed", I recommend that you watch it. And then tell me you wouldn't do that "yourself" but wouldn't object if someone else did.

That little child in the womb is a human being, created in the image and likeness of God. What possible reason could we have for taking her life away?

If we can take her life, whom else can we kill? Her parents are too poor to take care of her? Well, if we can kill her, what would be wrong with killing the *born* children of poor people? The only difference is where they live and how big they are. We have to abort her because she'll be handicapped? Why not kill the rest of the handicapped, too? Do they mean that little to us? Who are we to say she can't live because her life won't be up to our standards? She's unwanted? What about the homeless? Do we reach out in love to them or shoot them?

Abortion is supposed to solve the problems of women. But really, what does it solve? If a woman is poor, what does it solve to take her money, kill her child, and send her back to the slum? Nothing. It just kills her child. If a woman has been raped, does abortion un-rape her? No—it just kills her child. Face it—invading her body and killing her child cannot possibly be good for her, regardless of the problem.

Sure, there are problems that bring on abortion—big problems. Poverty, rape, incest—these aren't pretty. But does abortion bring us one step closer to solving them? No. Abortion gives us nothing but a dead child. It's an act of violence, nothing more. And a civilized society like ours should be able to solve our problems without resorting to violence against our own children. And to be "personally opposed" to that kind of violence is nothing but a cop-out. You can do better.

If someone were planning to kill *you*, you'd want people who care about you to be more than "personally opposed". You'd want them to do something about it. You'd want them to defend you. If you really want to love, and to respect human life, I suggest that you do the same.

23

Abortion: So It's Wrong.
What Am I Supposed to Do about It?

Those who respect life must accompany their teaching about the value of every human life with concrete and effective acts of solidarity to people in difficult situations. Without charity, the struggle to defend life would be lacking the essential ingredient of the Christian ethic; as St. Paul writes: "Do not be overcome with evil, but overcome evil with good."

— *John Paul II, Denver, 1993*

Woe to you if you do not succeed in defending life.

— *John Paul II, Denver, 1993*

Whoa!

We've all heard, "As long as you tried your best, whatever happens is okay", or "Give it your best shot, and then let the chips fall where they may." But the Pope is saying something completely different here. He's not saying we should try our best and then see what happens. He's not saying woe to us if we don't try. He's saying woe to us if we don't *succeed*. That's different!

"Cut us some slack", you say. "Do you know what

you're asking? There's a *lot* of abortion out here, and it's pretty well entrenched. This is a pretty big job here."

What does he mean? What does he expect of us? What is he saying?

Well, for starters, what does "woe" mean? According to Brother Webster, the dictionary guy, it means "grief, troubles, affliction". It means bad times, bummer ahead.

Basically, the Pope is saying that if we don't get rid of abortion, we've got bad times coming up. We're going to be miserable. We're going to have a lot of grief, trouble, and affliction.

That's not too hard to figure out. A society that kills 1.5 million innocent children every year obviously doesn't have much respect for life. And if they don't respect *all* human life, where does it end? We get rid of unborn babies because they're inconvenient. Who else is inconvenient? Old people, for starters. They need to be taken care of, they use up valuable medical treatment when they're just going to die anyway, and we're generally in a hurry to collect our inheritance before they get a chance to blow it all on doctors and pain killers. Why not get them out of the way, too?

Hey, what about poor people? They just take up space, right? What are they really contributing? And how about the handicapped? Maybe they could be expendable, too. And what about that ethnic group you don't really like? Or those Christians who are always making people feel so guilty?

If you think that lack of respect for life is going to stop with the unborn, guess again. It never works that way. It didn't work that way in Nazi Germany. They started with the unborn, the handicapped, and the old, and they ended by nearly exterminating an entire race.

We're already on our way. We have a nutcase doctor in Michigan killing people in the back of his van, and for a long time no one even tried to stop him. "Voluntary suicide" is now legal in the state of Oregon. In The Netherlands, where "mercy killing" is common, old people are afraid to go to the hospital. And here in the U.S., born handicapped babies have been left to starve because they weren't "good enough".

It's only going to get worse. Who else's life won't they respect? Your parents'? Your friends'? Your children's? Your own?

The Pope is saying that, if it comes down this way, it won't do a whole lot of good to say, "But, gee, I really *tried* to stop abortion." Trying is good, and we need to try as hard as we can. But if we try and lose, there'll be hell to pay.

To paraphrase a quote attributed to a post-war German citizen:

> When they came for the Poles, I said nothing, for I was not a Pole.
> When they came for the Gypsies, I said nothing, for I was not a Gypsy.
> When they came for the Jews, I said nothing, for I was not a Jew.
> When they came for me, no one said anything, for there was no one left.

If you want someone to be left when they come for you, I suggest you start working for the unborn now. Work hard—as though your life depended on it. Because it jolly well might.

How We *Don't* Defend Life—
Killing Abortion Doctors

I'm sure that any of you who are known among your friends as being pro-life have had to answer a lot of questions about the shootings at various abortion clinics. People are asking you to explain how, in the name of pro-*life*, someone can justify killing someone else. You see people on TV ranting and raving about how these pro-lifers are really a bunch of violent terrorists, and you're not too sure you even want to be known as pro-life any more. How *can* pro-lifers defend killing these guys?

They can't. And they haven't.

Pro-lifers, *real* pro-lifers who actually do respect human life, are appalled by what has happened. Every single national pro-life leader has denounced these types of killings in no uncertain terms. This is exactly what we're against. A real pro-lifer is the *last* person who would senselessly kill anyone. We're against violence. We're the ones outside trying to *stop* violence. We're the ones who want people to live.

Paul Hill, the guy who has been convicted of the murder of Dr. Britton, has supported the idea of killing abortion doctors for quite a while, saying that it's justified in a "war", and it's self-defense to protect those innocent children from a man who would kill them.

There's no doubt that Dr. Britton and Dr. Gunn were killing unborn children. And that's a very bad thing to do. A hideous thing. It's something they had no right to do. But even people who do hideous things have a right not to have their lives taken by individual vigilantes. To kill him was to play God—judge, jury, and executioner all rolled up into one.

Self-defense? The Church says that, in self-defense, if someone is in immediate danger, we have the right to exert as much force as is necessary to remove the danger. No more. What would it have taken to stop the danger? Sitting in front of the clinic's door could definitely be justified. Premeditated shooting to kill, however, can't be justified.

The biggest evil in abortion is not the fact that babies die. That's evil, all right, very evil, and man has no right to do that. But at least those babies go to a better place. The *biggest* evil is the eternal souls that are lost—people playing God take other lives, their hearts become hardened, and they risk losing their souls as a result. That's why we should pray for the souls of those who perform abortions.

What happened here? Men in the midst of sinful lives were shot in cold blood. Killing them didn't stop abortion. It probably didn't save one single life. Any woman planning to get an abortion could still go to any one of a jillion other doctors to have it done. But these men have been robbed of the chance to repent and to be reconciled with God. We can't know what happened to their souls —only God can judge that. But their lives should not have been taken, and they definitely should not have been taken by someone claiming to be "pro-life".

Bernard Nathanson—It's a Good Thing No One Ever Shot Him

There is another reason we might want to think twice about killing abortionists. Sometimes they end up helping us.

If there were ever an abortionist that a "pro-life" lunatic would want to kill, Bernard Nathanson would have been that abortionist. In the 1960s, when abortion wasn't even legal yet, he founded the National Association for the Repeal of Abortion Laws (now the National Abortion Rights Action League—NARAL).

His organization decided that, in order to create sympathy for their cause, they needed to identify an "enemy" to be the bad guy so that they could look like good guys. The enemy they targeted? The Roman Catholic Church. They used the media to create a massive propaganda campaign painting the Catholic Church as male-dominated, cruel, and opposed to abortion out of insensitivity to women. They portrayed themselves, on the other hand, as loving, sensitive to women, and in favor of abortion.

Despite the fact that the Catholic Church does far more for women in crisis pregnancy than any other agency in the world, they were successful. Anti-Catholicism still rears its ugly head in the abortion debate on a regular basis. (When was the last time you heard of a prolife congressman identified as a "Methodist" or "Presbyterian"? But if he's Catholic, you'd better bet it'll be pointed out every time his name is mentioned.)

They were successful in other ways, too. They wanted people to believe that a lot of women died every year of illegal abortions, to convince people that legal abortion would save women's lives. Problem was, after the advent of penicillin, not enough women died of illegal abortions to scare people. In 1972, for example, the year before *Roe v Wade*, thirty-nine women died as a result of illegal abortion. They didn't think that was enough. So they made up numbers. *Huge* numbers. They claimed that up to ten thousand women were dying every year, all from illegal abortion. They lied, and Dr. Nathanson admits it.

And it worked. Those numbers still show up in debates on an appallingly regular basis, despite the absolute lack of verification. Rarely are the numbers questioned. People were, and still are, ridiculously gullible.

And then Dr. Nathanson did more. When abortion was made legal in New York in 1969, he opened the largest abortion clinic in the nation. There, and in other settings, he presided over sixty thousand abortions.

Not a real likable guy.

They claimed that up to ten thousand women were dying every year, all from illegal abortion. They lied, and Dr. Nathanson admits it.

But then something happened to Dr. Bernard Nathanson. His conscience. It began to bother him. He began to question his involvement in abortion. He wrote a book called *Aborting America*, admitting that he'd lied, admitting that the unborn child was more than just a "clump of cells", admitting that modern ultrasound showed us, for the first time, a very vital, alive child, even at the earliest abortions.

When Bernard Nathanson became pro-life, he did it in a big way. Through his organization, Bernadell, he produced *Eclipse of Reason* and *The Silent Scream,* two of the most powerful pro-life videos ever made. He wrote a second book, *The Abortion Papers*, detailing his lies, deceptions, and manipulation in working to legalize abortion and showing how the abortion movement still lies, deceives, and manipulates. He became involved in Operation Rescue and was arrested several times. He continues to work and speak tirelessly for the pro-life movement. He has no doubt saved countless, countless babies.

It's a good thing no one shot him.

Bernard Nathanson is not the only one. The Pro-Life Action League sponsors a "Meet the Abortion Providers" conference every year, where former abortionists who are now pro-life activists gather and speak on how to influence abortionists to stop and on how to stop abortion.

David Gunn—On His Way Out of the Abortion Business?

I spoke with a good friend of mine who is a national leader in the pro-life movement. He told me that many people, including a former abortionist who knew him, believe that Dr. David Gunn was actually on the verge of quitting the abortion business when he was killed. He had already stopped doing late-term abortions because he knew the baby felt pain, and his conscience bothered him. Who knows where his conscience would have taken him next? Maybe, by this time, he would've been working with former abortionists like Bernard Nathanson, working to undo the damage he'd done.

We'll never know, will we?

Killers Aren't Pro-life

Naturally, the pro-abortion forces are using this to try to convince people that all pro-lifers are violent, which is ludicrous. Every single social movement in history, from women's liberation to the civil rights movement, has had what we call a "lunatic fringe". People who tend to be unbalanced are often attracted to causes. I guess a lunatic alone is just a lunatic, but a lunatic for a cause can convince himself he's a hero. And so acts of senseless violence have always been committed in the name of social movements, no matter how noble the cause.

The difference is that, with other causes, people are smart enough to recognize that the movement itself isn't responsible for the violence of individual lunatics. Paul Hill, for instance, was never a "pro-life leader". No one really knew who he was. He was just a guy who showed up at a couple of meetings and got a lot of attention by screaming that abortionists should die. Pro-lifers who are putting their lives on the line to save others don't deserve to be lumped in with him. But being pro-life is so un-popular that some people want to believe we're violent. I guess it's easier than listening to what we have to say.

Pro-life means just that. Pro-life. It means we respect all life, not just the lives we like. A real pro-lifer brings that respect into his everyday life and to *all* of his pro-life work.

Don't give up your pro-life work. Don't be afraid to tell people where you stand. Just make sure that, in you, they see what a pro-life person is *really* like.

Remember, "they'll know we are Christians by our love"—not by our guns.

So How *Do* We Defend Life?

Enough about how we *don't* defend life. What *can* we do?

Obviously, we need to work to stop abortion. As John

Paul II says, woe to us if we don't succeed. The question is, how do we succeed?

There are a lot of ways. Pro-life activity breaks down into four different areas: legislation, education, direct action, and direct aid. Different people are good at different things, and they will probably be attracted to different areas of pro-life activism. And that's a good thing. We wouldn't get very far if everyone were doing the same thing. The point is to do *something* to defend life, and among these four areas, there's sure to be something you can do. So let's look at them:

1. *Legislation*

When the Supreme Court decision *Roe v Wade* was handed down, it took the country completely by surprise. At that time, abortion was illegal in most states and available under limited circumstances in the rest. But all of that changed, literally overnight.

Under *Roe v Wade*, abortion is legal in the U.S. throughout all nine months of pregnancy. In most states, minor girls can obtain abortions without their parents' consent, yet those same girls can't be given aspirin or have their ears pierced without parental permission. Abortions are easier to get in this country than anywhere else in the world. This is a travesty.

There's plenty a young, civic-minded individual can do to further the cause of legal protection for the unborn. Do volunteer work for a local pro-life candidate. If there's pro-life legislation being introduced in your community, contact the sponsors and help them distribute leaflets or gather signatures. Talk to your voting-age friends about the importance of voting pro-life.

2. *Education*

Even if abortion were to be made illegal tomorrow, we'd still have a problem. We have an entire generation that has never known a society where abortion wasn't legal. The legality, and the acceptability, of abortion on demand is etched into their consciousness. They've always heard that abortion is a woman's "right", so they figure it must be true.

The average American has no idea how abortions are performed or what is done to the unborn child. They've been told that the child is just a "blob of tissue", and they believe it. We need to change that. We need to show them, every time and in every way we can, that the unborn child is a living, moving, thumb-sucking, pain-feeling person at the time of the very earliest abortions. We need to show them the cruel abortion methods that literally rip a human person limb from limb.

How do we show them? Several ways. First of all, learn the facts of fetal development yourself. Dr. Wilke's book *Abortion Questions and Answers* is very helpful for this and other abortion-related matters. Learn about abortion methodology. If you really want the gory details, buy a video like *The Silent Scream*, *Eclipse of Reason*, or *Hard Truth*. (Your local pro-life organization can tell you where to get them.)

And then, once you know the facts, share them. Talk to your friends about it. If you really want to share the word, contact your local pro-life groups about getting onto a speakers' bureau and giving talks on abortion in schools. Write an article for your school paper.

And while we're talking about education, abortion education isn't the only kind we need. If we're going to get to the root of the problem, we need to get rid of the *demand* for abortion. And to do that, we need chastity education. We need to help people figure out how to respect their sexual capacity so that they're using it at the service of real love, instead of abusing it at the expense of the next generation's lives. So spread the word on that, too!

Even if you aren't directly involved in pro-life education, it's absolutely crucial that you be well versed on the issues. You don't have to be standing in front of an audience to have your views on abortion challenged. It'll happen all the time—with your friends, at parties, anywhere people manage to find out that you're Catholic. You can use those opportunities to clear up some ignorance and make a difference in people's lives, *if* you know what you're talking about.

3. *Direct Action*

What would you do if you knew there was a house in your neighborhood where people were killed on a regular basis? Maybe you'd tell the police and try to get the house closed down. But what would you do in the meantime? If you saw someone walking in, would you warn them? Of course you would.

There *are* lives being threatened today, in your very own neighborhood, at your local abortion facility. Someone needs to act *now*, to save the lives most immediately threatened by abortion. That's direct action.

There are a lot of ways you can make an impact on your local abortion facility. One way is picketing and sidewalk counseling. It's not too tough to stand outside a clinic with a sign, or to walk up to the women going in and offer them help. Most women don't *want* to have abortions. They feel trapped—they think they have no other options. You can be there for them at the last minute, to let them know that they *do* have options and that you'll help them find them.

Of course, all of these activities have gotten tougher since clinics have started using escorts (or "deathscorts", as they're known) to hustle their "clients" into the building before you can even talk to them. But, even in the presence of deathscorts, your presence outside can be extremely effective.

Direct action and peaceful protest have also been complicated by recent legislation establishing "bubble zones" around abortion facilities. But these laws don't mean you have to stay home. The bubble zone has to end somewhere. Just stay outside of it. Check with your local pro-life organization to see how the laws are applied in your area.

Direct action is usually popular with pro-life students, because they often see direct results and really feel as if they're *doing* something. But, in direct action, there are often results you don't see. Former abortionists report that when there was even one picket sign outside, abortions inside decreased by half. Women ask more questions, many drive away without even going in, many walk out before the abortion is performed.

Of course, in direct action, as in everything else, the guiding principle should be love. Don't carry vicious signs or yell obnoxiously at women going in. Would that change your mind? It probably won't change theirs, either. Show them that you're someone who really cares about them and who has a better way. They'll see that and respond.

4. *Direct Aid*

Direct action without direct aid is hypocrisy. Women who seek abortions are often in really desperate situations. The abortion doesn't solve their problems—it just kills their children. But how much good are we doing them if we just say, "Go home. Don't have an abortion. It'll all be fine"?

People sometimes accuse us of being "fetus-lovers" and not caring about women at all. Of course, that isn't true. I don't want women to have abortions, because it hurts them *and* their children. Killing a woman's child can't be good for her. Anyone who knows someone who's been through an abortion can attest to that. That's why pro-life means loving them *both*.

That's the idea behind pro-life pregnancy centers. These centers do a lot more than help a woman understand why she shouldn't have an abortion. They are places where she can get real help, help that she and her baby can both live with. The services are free, no one's making any money off of her (unlike the abortion industry), and the people there really do care about her and want to help.

And they can help. Centers offer everything from baby clothes to parenting classes to welfare referrals. Some even offer prenatal care. And they offer something even more important—emotional support. Sometimes a woman just needs someone to stand by her and be her friend when everyone else is pressuring her to abort. The counselors at these centers strive to be there for her, for whatever she needs.

There's a lot you could do for your local pro-life pregnancy center. They always need counselors as well as other help. And they usually have excellent training programs. And they'd love to see bright, eager young faces at their doors. So give them a call!

With all of these ideas, I'm sure there's *something* you could be doing to help John Paul II "defend life". Whatever you do, do *something*, because someday you'll face God, and He'll probably point out to you that there was a huge slaughter going in your day. Young innocents were killed, right in your own neighborhood. He'll be interested to hear just what you did to stop it.

And I don't think "I was too busy" is going to be an adequate answer.

24

Should Christians Be Environmentalists?

Likewise, false models of progress have led to endangering the earth's proper ecological balance. Man—made in the image and likeness of the Creator—was meant to be the Good Shepherd of the environment in which he exists and lives. This is an ancient task, which the human family carried out with fair success down through history, until in recent times man himself has become the destroyer of his own natural environment.

— John Paul II, Denver, 1993

At last—a way to be Christian and popular at the same time! By getting involved in protecting the environment, you can do the right thing and still be politically correct!

Hold on. Before you run off to get your Greenpeace card, let's take a little closer look at this whole issue of environmental protection. The environmental movement is probably one of the largest social movements of the late twentieth century. And, as John Paul II points out, it is in many ways a very important movement. But we need to understand *why* it's important and what should motivate us to protect the environment.

When God plopped us here on Earth, he didn't just

set us up in some functional but boring place, like the administration building of the average campus. He gave us an extraordinarily beautiful Earth. Have you ever seen the California coast, or the Colorado Rockies at sunset, or New England in the fall? This is a gorgeous set-up we're living in. But it doesn't come to us without a certain price. God has given us a *huge* responsibility here on Earth—we're supposed to take care of the place. It's only fair—we'll be here only for a while, but the world will have to last for generations to come. The least we can do is to clean up before the next tenants arrive.

Unfortunately, the rapid technological progress of recent generations hasn't always respected the integrity and beauty of God's creation. Twentieth-century man figured out that there are a whole lot of ways we can make our lives more efficient. That's not a bad thing, but sometimes our search for speed and efficiency has taken a significant toll on the environment in which we live. That's bad.

I've lived in several major cities in the U.S., and I've visited most of the rest of them. There really are few sights in this world more disgusting than filthy, polluted air hanging over a city's skyline. The mere thought of that air actually going into someone's lungs is sickening.

God created the world to work as a unified whole. Trees emit the oxygen we need to breathe. We emit carbon dioxide that trees need. Animals prey on each other to maintain a natural balance. This is all part of the "proper ecological balance" that the Holy Father is talking about. Everything works together, and if one part gets too far out of kilter, it upsets the rest of the system.

So working to protect the beauty and integrity of God's creation is a good thing. Does that mean you can join any environmental group you find, confident that it will reflect the Christian values of stewardship of the earth?

Not necessarily. It's important to protect the earth, but it's also important to understand *why* we're doing it. This is where the Christian understanding of environmentalism differs from that of some of the more radical environmental groups.

For us, protecting the Earth is a part of loving each other. The Earth was created by God so that people, created in His image and likeness, could have a beautiful place to live, eat, thrive, and work out God's plan. It was given to us, for our use and our enjoyment. We need to protect it and to maintain the proper ecological balance, so that others of our generation and the generations to come can use and enjoy it, too. The Earth is for man, and we protect it for the sake of man.

The Christian viewpoint has certain ramifications. Protection of the environment obviously isn't an absolute. We don't say we should never chop down a tree. Our appreciation of trees is mitigated by our appreciation of having houses to live in and tables to eat on. We need a certain amount of progress to protect our lives and our interests. And while as Christians we shouldn't be cruel to animals, neither should we put their welfare above the welfare of people created in God's image. Our struggle is in finding a balance that gives us progress without unduly harming or sacrificing the other elements of God's creation.

Some of the more radical environmentalists, however, have a different philosophy. They don't believe that the

Earth is for man. They believe that man is for the Earth. To them the Earth itself is more important than the human people God placed in it.

This philosophy also has ramifications. To them, if a conflict arises between what's best for the natural environment or animals and what's best for people, they will defend the natural environment—even at the expense of the good of human persons. They believe that, if man is getting in the way of the Earth or of animals, then man should get out of the way.

We protect the Earth for the sake of God's highest creation, human beings.

The philosophy of the radical environmentalists is based on a misunderstanding of truth and of God's "value system". God created man above the animals—we have eternal souls, we're created in His image and likeness. The Earth has value because it serves us and allows us to fulfill our mission in this world. We protect the Earth for the sake of God's highest creation, human beings. Radical environmentalists, on the other hand, value trees, animals, and scenery for their own sake, giving them more value than the humans who use and enjoy them. They've set up a sort of false "religion" that puts the creation ahead of the Creator. To sacrifice human well-being to protect a tree or an animal is to distort the truth of God's creation.

Even within the Christian philosophy of environmental protection, there is a lot of room for disagreement. How much progress should we allow? How much open space should we leave? Does it better serve man to have more national parks or more office parks? These are issues on which good Christians can and do disagree—sometimes very vocally. But they need to agree on the final goal—protecting the Earth for the sake of the humans who inhabit it.

Go ahead—be an environmentalist. Be the best environmentalist you can be. Protect God's creation. But don't forget *why* you're protecting it. You're protecting it because God created you and everyone else in His image and likeness. He loves us immensely, and He wants us to protect each other. Part of that protection is protecting our home. But it's only part of that protection, not all of it.

Remember that people come first.

25

Why Is Life So Unfair Sometimes?

It is true that young people today experience difficulties that previous generations experienced only partially and in a limited way.

— *John Paul II, Manila, 1995*

Take courage in the face of life's difficulties and injustices. Commit yourselves to the struggle for justice, solidarity, and peace in the world.

— *John Paul II, Denver, 1993*

Don't you hate suffering? I do. I'd much rather be happy than miserable. In fact, I'm capable of going to great lengths to avoid anything even remotely unpleasant.

Evangelization, unfortunately, tends to contain a certain element of suffering. Look where it got Jesus. Most of his followers died in similar ways. We may not be crucified, but if we work for a better world or to spread the good news, we're risking our popularity, our status, and our comfort. It won't always be easy.

We all know that life has a significant element of suffering to it even before we start evangelizing. Life always has valleys as well as peaks. Sometimes I think that, in a certain sense, teenage suffering is worse, because teens are going through it for the first time. By their fifth or sixth breakup, they realize that the world doesn't have to end with the relationship and that life goes on. But the first time, they're not so sure. The first time someone close to them dies, they have to deal not only with that loss but with that initial, brutal realization that life is fleeting and their loved ones won't be around forever. Add to this the fact that they have quarts of raging hormones playing havoc with their moods, that the world often seems to be a fairly screwed up place, and the fact that adults never seem to take their suffering seriously, and teen life isn't always a bowl of cherries. Teen highs are high, but the lows can be pretty low.

So what do we do when we're suffering? How do we handle the misery that comes with the breakup of a relationship or a family, or the realization that the world is full of injustice, or a hormone-induced depression? Our first reaction is to feel sorry for ourselves. "Woe is me, I'm suffering" was my usual attitude. We spend a lot of time *thinking* about our suffering and how miserable we are. We wallow in it.

The next step is usually to try to escape the suffering. We live in a world of remote control and Advil. Anything that causes us inconvenience or pain needs to be eliminated from our lives. We're not *supposed* to suffer. Life is supposed to be ease and convenience and beer on the beach. And so we dedicate ourselves to getting rid of the suffering, to *feeling* better. We drink. We distract ourselves with TV or shopping. We seek comfort in sexual relationships.

But John Paul II shows us a different way to handle the sufferings we encounter in life. "Take courage." Whoa, what a concept. Courage? What does it mean to take courage? It means we don't run away, that we face up. Courage doesn't try to escape suffering at any price; it faces it head on and moves forward toward the good, even if there's suffering along the way.

They lie when they tell us we aren't supposed to suffer in this life. It can be good to suffer, if we face suffering courageously. Suffering teaches us to rely on God. It gives us strength to strive for what's best, instead of just what's easiest. It allows us to join our sufferings to those of Christ, who certainly didn't run away from pain. He accepted a most hideous form of suffering—hanging from a cross by holes in his hands and dying. He could have gotten out of it, but He didn't, because there was a greater good to be gained—our redemption. When we suffer, we can join it to His suffering and use it to bring grace to a world that desperately needs it.

If we want to spread the gospel, if we want to struggle for solidarity, justice, and peace in the world, if we want to defend life, we have to expect to suffer some. Injustice, disunity, and fighting are far more popular in many quarters, and you won't be popular for standing up for politically incorrect causes like protecting the unborn. That's why the Holy Father calls it "struggling" for justice and not "partying" for justice. It's not easy to stand up for what's right. And if you've made a habit of drowning or fleeing every suffering moment that's come your way, you're not going to have the courage to stand up when the going gets rough.

Does this mean that God likes to see us suffer? No, He loves us, and love never enjoys the suffering of another. But like a parent who has to watch a doctor perform a painful procedure on a child, God knows that sometimes suffering will result in something good for us. And just as a parent watches a child suffer the consequences of his own mistakes, God knows that we, or those around us, often make stupid moves that cause us unhappiness. He never said He'd deliver us from stupidity or its consequences.

There's no such thing as a life without suffering. The question is, what are you going to do about it? Are you going to look at it and run the other way? Or are you going to face up to it and work through it to create a better situation? The inconveniences and tragedies of life aren't fun. But, if you let Him, God will use them as raw material. If we face up to our suffering with courage and go forward with God's will anyway, He'll use our difficulties to help us become better, stronger, holier people.

Doesn't that help make it all worthwhile?

26

Ask Not If Your Country Can Pray for You. . . .

America needs much prayer—lest it lose its soul.

— John Paul II, Denver, 1993

We've talked a lot about what trouble our country is in. We've talked about the lack of respect for life, a situation that's slowly eroding the fiber of our moral fabric. We've talked about all kinds of things we can do to make the world a better place—from cleaning up the air to spreading the gospel.

I'm sure we could talk about a million *more* things we could do for America. Help the homeless. Visit the sick. Balance the budget. There are a *lot* of problems out there, and sometimes it all seems really overwhelming. The problems are *huge* . Violence on the streets, gangs, euthanasia, child abuse, sexual harassment—the list goes on and on. What can you, as one person, really do? What can a lot of us working together really do? It just seems so hopeless sometimes.

John Paul II sees it, too. That's one reason he came here in 1993. He knows we're having a lot of problems. And he knows that we tend to export our problems. Everyone follows America, so our problems soon become other countries' problems. That's bad.

He said that America is in danger of "losing its soul". What does that mean? To be blunt, it means our country is going to hell. In a hand basket. Not literally, of course, as a country. But in a very real sense, nonetheless.

What does it mean when someone loses his soul? The soul is the center, the "core" of a person. It's what infuses your body and gives you life. God created our souls to be filled up with God, connected to Him. But what if we turn away from Him? Our souls, the core of our being, become isolated from God. In a very real way, things start to fall apart. We're unable to love as we should. Peace is gone. We become selfish and bitter. Finally, if we fail to repent and reconcile with God before we die, we've turned away from Him forever. It's a bad scene.

What does it mean when someone loses his soul?

That scenario isn't just played out for individuals. Something very similar can and does happen on a national level. A country has a sort of corporate "soul". At the core of its being, a country has an orientation—either toward God or away from God. You may have heard (unless your school took all the references to God out of the textbooks) that this country was once pretty well oriented to God. Our founding documents ooze phrases like "One nation, under God" and "In God we trust." Up until 1962, there was actually prayer in public schools.

Amazing, isn't it? Hard to believe now. Today, it'd be pretty tough to pray in the schools. A lot of people don't believe in God, and among the ones who do, you're not really sure whom exactly they mean by "god".

But our forefathers knew something that we seem to have forgotten. They knew that we don't hold things together. God does. And if we want a loving, peaceful society, if we want a society that works, we need God. We need Him badly. We need to stay close to Him, and we need His action in our lives—national as well as individual.

How do we improve America? Plenty of ways. We work for peace. We help the homeless. We fight for the right to life for the defenseless.

But more important than any of that is prayer. We need to pray. If we don't, all of our other efforts will be in vain. Things are a mess here, and as helpful as our efforts might be, alone they're not going to be enough. This is a job for God.

We don't often think of praying for our country. Prayer is for begging God for a C on your algebra test, or maybe thanking Him for giving you nice parents. We rarely take prayer out of the realm of our own personal lives and into the larger picture. But it belongs there.

Pray for America. Pray daily for our country and for our leaders. They have a lot to do, and some of them aren't doing such a hot job. They need all of the divine assistance they can get. Pray for the people in our country who are in trouble, or who don't know God, or who are fighting Him.

And then go out and do something. Prayer isn't necessarily a substitute for action. But if your action is supported and informed by prayer, you'll have a better idea what you need to do, and you'll be more successful. Because it won't just be your action. You and God will be working as a team.

Prayer is the only way to win. And when the stakes are this high, you don't want to lose.

27

To Whom Can I Turn When I Really Need a Friend?

At Holy Ghost Church your pilgrimage will lead you to Christ in the blessed Eucharist. In prayer before the Blessed Sacrament exposed you can pour out your hearts to Him, but especially you must listen to what He has to say to each one of you. Christ's favorite words to young people are "Fear not" (Mt 10:31) and "Come, follow me" (Mt 19:21).

— John Paul II, Denver, 1993

Jesus Christ wants to be your "friend". He wants to be your "companion" at every stage of the road of life. He wants to be the "way", your path through the anxieties, doubts, hopes, and dreams of happiness.

— John Paul II, Manila, 1995

I invite you to create a climate of silence and reflection, so that a deepening awareness of the mystery can grow in every young person gathered here. Let us pray that the love which God pours into our hearts through the Holy Spirit may not be blocked or hindered by passing distractions.

— John Paul II, Denver, 1993

When something is really wrong, or when you really need to talk, whom do you go to? Your parents? Your best friend? Your boyfriend or girlfriend?

What is it about those people that draws you to them? Maybe it's because they know you better than anyone else. Maybe it's because they love you, and you know they'll care about what's going on in your life, and they'll look out for what's best for you. Maybe it's because they're really wise and give great advice.

It's great to have someone to talk to, and everyone needs someone like that. But, unfortunately, people have their limits. They don't *totally* know you, they can't *always* be there for you, and they don't *always* know the answers. So, even though our friends can be a big help, we're generally still left with our problems.

Wouldn't it be nice to have a friend who wasn't limited by human constraints; a companion who knew you better than you know yourself, who loved you more than you love yourself, and who always had the answers? I'd pay big bucks to talk to someone like that.

We have Someone like that, and He's right under our noses, so to speak. When we go into a Catholic church, God is present there. Physically present.

What does it mean for God to be "physically present"? Some people say, "Sure God is present there. God is everywhere . . . in the breeze, and in the flowers. . . ." But that's not it. We've already talked about how we believe that, in the Eucharist, Jesus Christ is fully, physically present—body, blood, soul, and divinity. The whole Jesus. That's why there's a candle lit near the tabernacle when the Eucharist is present and why we genuflect. We're acknowledging that He's there and showing Him honor and respect.

We go to Mass to receive Him in the Eucharist. But it's important to remember that He's *always* there, not just during Mass. While we're at Mass, we need to acknowledge that fact. And it doesn't hurt to visit Him every once in a while when there's no Mass going on. It's nice that way—just you and God, together for a little chat.

So what are we supposed to do in His presence? Pray. What does that mean? Say "Our Fathers" and "Hail Marys"? That's a great start; prayers like that are important. But is that all? The Holy Father tells us that, in prayer before the Blessed Sacrament, we can "pour out our hearts to Him". Prayer is quite simply communication with God, the God who knows you and loves you better than anyone. He wants you to talk to Him, from the heart. He wants to be your "path through the anxieties, doubts, hopes, and dreams of happiness". He wants you to come to Him with your problems. If you're sad, He wants to hear about it. If you're mad, He wants to hear about it. And He wouldn't mind hearing about the good times, either.

"Talking to God is nice", you say. "But He doesn't talk back."

He wants you to come to Him with your problems. If you're sad, He wants to hear about it. If you're mad, He wants to hear about it. And He wouldn't mind hearing about the good times, either.

A few years ago, I spoke at a youth rally in Los Angeles. During the cross-talk, one girl stood up and said, "To be perfectly honest, I don't turn to God when I have a problem. I mean, your friends can talk back. God doesn't *talk* to us."

It's easy to feel that way sometimes. Especially when you're lonely or upset, you want to *hear* from someone. And, for that particular request, God doesn't seem to fit the bill.

But John Paul II doesn't see it that way. "You must listen to what He has to say to each one of you." He talks back!! He has a specific message for each individual and each situation. And He brings that message to us, not generally in the midst of the noise of our lives, but in the quiet of prayer.

"Yeah, right", you say. "How come *I've* never heard this message. He doesn't speak to me." Well, how can you be so sure?

How do you suppose God speaks to you? If you're waiting for Him to call you on the phone, or send you a fax, or maybe get you on e-mail, you'll be waiting a long time. God's not a real high-tech kind of God. Moses got a burning bush, but God doesn't use those much any more. Environmental laws probably cramped his style. According to John Paul II, God prefers more traditional, provincial ways of communicating. He speaks in "a climate of silence and reflection".

It's no wonder you haven't heard from Him lately. How much silence is there in your life? How much silence is there in any of our lives? When was the last time you were *anywhere*, alone, without the radio or MTV blaring at you? When was the last time you were listening for what God had to say? Without that silence, you'll miss His message.

"Fear Not!"

The Holy Father says that God speaks to us when we find silent time, prayer time, to be with him. When we are silent and He does speak, one of His favorite things to say to us is "Fear not!"

"Fear not" is the kind of thing a lot of people say. "Oh, don't worry. Everything will be okay." "Relax—it'll all work out." That generally isn't very comforting, is it? How do *they* know everything will be okay? They have no idea what will happen. They're usually just saying that because they don't know what else to say, and they want you to feel better.

But when *God* tells you not to be afraid, He knows what He's talking about. He *knows* what's coming up. He knows exactly what will happen to you, and He *controls* what happens to you. When He says, "Fear not!", you know He means it. That's comforting.

The best thing about going to God when we're afraid or when we have problems is that He can actually do something to help. He tells us "Ask, and you shall receive; seek and you shall find; knock and it shall be opened to you" (Lk 11:10). He doesn't say, "I'll automatically help" or "Ignore Me, and you shall receive." He wants us to go to Him, probably to remind us that He loves us and that He's the one in control.

The difference between going to God with our problems and going to our friend is that God, being wiser than even our smartest friends, knows exactly what we need. The tricky part is, it may not be what we think we need. At those times it may seem as if He's not listening. I can't begin to tell you the number of times I've gone before God with some intention that I desperately wanted, only to be disappointed. It was often only with years of hindsight that I could see that not getting what I wanted was exactly what I needed. What I wanted at that particular time would have caused me huge problems in the long run. God had actually answered my prayer, far beyond my wildest expectations. I've had to face facts. He's a lot smarter than I am. I might as well just trust Him.

We can pray anywhere. But there's a special power and beauty in going to God in the Blessed Sacrament, to spend some quiet time alone with Him. There's something about His physical presence that brings Him concretely into our lives—especially when we really need to hear that "Fear not!"

In 1990, I was diagnosed with malignant melanoma, a particularly deadly form of skin cancer. I was terrified. That evening, I went to church and prayed before the Blessed Sacrament. And I heard the "Fear not!" that John Paul II is talking about. I *knew* that God was with me and that, whether I was cured or not, He would remain beside me and take loving care of me. I found a tremendous, almost supernatural calm in His healing presence. That calm didn't leave me when I walked out of that church but lasted throughout my treatment.

"Fear not!" doesn't necessarily mean that nothing will ever go wrong or that everything will go the way you want it to. But it means, as I realized, that He is with us no matter what, and in His love, He gives us a strength and a peace that will allow us to weather any storm, and to do it all with a peace and a serenity that surpasses any human understanding.

Awareness of the Mystery

"Fear not!" isn't the only thing that God has to say to us. He also gives us an awareness of the "mystery". What is this "mystery" the Pope is talking about? It's the mystery of redemption—the fact that Christ died on the Cross to save us from our sins.

I know that ever since you were a little kid, you've probably been beaten over the head with "Jesus died on the Cross for you, so don't hit your brother after Mass." But now that you're older, it's a good time to "reflect" on the redemption in a little more adult way. When we see the crucifix at church, it looks kind of antiseptic. Jesus is hanging up there, a little blood flowing from his hands and feet. They cleaned it up. The real crucifixion was way too gross to depict in a pleasant place like church. Christ was a bloody, pulpy mess. He was whipped until most of his skin was gone and then hung by holes in his hands and feet. They say He died because of the strain of it all. It was a cruel, hideous, torturous death.

Reflect for a minute on why God went through that. He's God, you know. He didn't have to. He didn't have to become a man at all. It would have been a lot easier just to stay in heaven, where the weather's always good, and everyone is always nice. He wouldn't have had to deal with half-witted disciples who never quite grasped what he was talking about. And, in heaven, He certainly wouldn't have had to deal with unpleasant realities like crucifixion.

So what good does it do us to have an "awareness" of this mystery of Christ's crucifixion? Simple. He went through all of that pain and torture because He loves you. Yes, you. That bloody, pulpy mess of a death restored our relationships with God. Sure, He could've done it an easier way. He's God. He could just have said, "Aw, forget about Adam and Eve. Let's just start over. What do you say?" But that wouldn't have shown us how much He loved us, would it? Dying for us—now that really says something.

John Paul II says that, in silence and reflection, God gives us a deeper awareness of this mystery. What do we become aware of? His amazing love for us—a love that would offer up His life. His amazing concern for us. We become aware of our incredible value in His eyes. Other people's opinions of us mean less in the light of God's opinion—He thought we were worth dying for.

And He does more yet. He pours love into our hearts. He gives us that real love, the one that comes straight from the manufacturer of love Himself. In a loveless world, that's a gift worth seeking out.

The Holy Father says that love and awareness can be blocked by passing distractions. It's easy for all of us to get distracted. Life can be very busy. Between work and school and sports and clubs and friends and family, sometimes it's hard to find time to sleep, much less reflect. But try to put it into perspective. Can we really afford to let those distractions block our communication with God? What could be more important than learning about God's love for you? I can always find the time to listen to someone who loves me. And if that Someone loved me enough to die for me, I think I'd have an awful lot of time to listen.

Do you know anyone with too much love in their life? Neither do I. We all want love. We *need* love to survive. So none of us can afford to miss out on the love God is sending our way. We need to make the time to be with Him, to listen to what He has to say to us.

Many churches have special times of adoration, where the Blessed Sacrament is exposed for adoration and prayer. Others have perpetual adoration, where a special room is reserved for constant exposition and adoration. *All* Catholic churches have the Blessed Sacrament present, whether in the main church or in a special eucharistic chapel. Find out what your neighborhood parishes offer. Take advantage of that time.

Whether you pray in His presence in church or in the privacy of your own room, the important thing is that you pray—every day. I know it's easy to get distracted. But He has something to say to you, and I know you have plenty to say to Him. This is a relationship you can't afford to let slide.

Lose the distractions. Make the time.

28

How Does My Relationship with God Affect My Relationships with My Friends?

It is He, Jesus Christ, the true life, who gives hope and purpose to our earthly existence, opens our minds and hearts to the goodness and beauty of the world around us, to solidarity and friendship with our fellow human beings, to intimate communion with God Himself, in a love that goes beyond all limits of time and space, to eternal, unassailable happiness.

— *John Paul II, Denver, 1993*

Have you ever had a friendship, or a moment in a friendship, when you felt touched by something supernatural? Maybe you just had a really good talk, or a really good cry with a friend. Maybe you just patched up a disagreement. Maybe you had a lot of fun together. But in real intimacy, whether between friends or lovers (in the chaste sense, of course), there are occasional, beautiful moments when you realize the incredible preciousness of this relationship, and you feel the presence of something almost magical.

What you're experiencing at those times isn't "magic", and it isn't just in your mind. You're experiencing the presence of Jesus Christ, who "opens our minds . . . to solidarity and friendship with our fellow human beings". God is love, the Author of love, and wherever you find genuine love, you find Him. God comes to us through our human relationships, through human love.

When I was in college, we spent a lot of time studying the ancient Greek philosopher, Aristotle, whom I didn't particularly expect to enjoy. But, amazingly enough, I learned more about things that are important to me, like friendship, from Aristotle than from anyone else. (Ironic, huh? Learning about friendship from a dead Greek guy. It's kind of like learning about sex from the Pope. Sometimes the least likely sources turn out to be the best.)

Aristotle said that friendship is always based on some common goal or interest. Friendship among thieves is based on the fact that they all like to steal things. Friendships among teammates are based on a common love of the sport. Aristotle said that the higher the goal or interest shared, the closer and more beautiful the friendship. To Aristotle, the highest type of friendship was a friendship based on virtue. But then again, Aristotle never knew Jesus Christ.

Have you ever had a friendship with someone who shared your faith? If you have, you've seen what Aristotle means. There can be beauty and magic in a lot of different friendships, but there's a special intimacy and an ease in friendships based on a shared spiritual life. There's an ability to talk freely and openly about the deepest, most important part of your life in Christ without having to explain. And your common goal goes far beyond winning a game. Your goal is heaven and "eternal, unassailable happiness".

Those of you who've been to one of the World Youth Day events experienced this. You were all surrounded by hundreds of thousands of others who shared your faith and your love for Christ and His vicar, John Paul II. The camaraderie is always amazing during those times, and instant friendships spring up everywhere. There is a spirit of incredible unity and love among all of the participants. It's as if everyone already knows each other. It's no wonder. When your love is based on the Author of love, it's going to be easier to do it right.

We all need friendships based on faith. Now, I'm not saying we need to retreat into a "Catholic ghetto" where we refuse to associate with anyone who doesn't share our faith. For one thing, that would be a pretty small ghetto. There just aren't that many of us around sometimes. But, beyond that, we're each called to be a "light on the hill" and bring Christ to others. We can't do that if we associate only with people who already know Him.

But neither can we do it if our own faith isn't being nourished. It's difficult enough to follow Christ in this day and age. It's practically impossible without some peer support. Our own faith needs to grow, develop, and thrive, and it's tough to do that alone. Without some support, others will influence us more easily than we influence others.

John Paul II said that Christ leads us "to solidarity and friendship with our fellow human beings, to intimate communion with God Himself, in a love that goes beyond all limits of time and space, to eternal, unassailable happiness". His phrasing was no accident. Friendship in Christ leads us to intimate communion with God and to eternal happiness. Our real friends bring us closer to God and bring us a foretaste of the "eternal, unassailable happiness" of heaven. I know my friends do that. They are a precious gift from God, and I'm eternally grateful for them.

And if you and your friends all help each other persevere in Christ throughout your lives, then your friendships don't ever have to end. You can spend eternity together, praising God and reminiscing about the "old days" on Earth.

My wish for you is that you, too, can find and experience friendships in Christ. Friends who share faith are an incredible gift in this life, and they help us to prepare for what really matters—the life to come. And if you and your friends all help each other persevere in Christ throughout your lives, then your friendships don't ever have to end. You can spend eternity together, praising God and reminiscing about the "old days" on Earth.

What about Friends Who *Aren't* in Christ?

We've talked about how good friendships can lead you to Christ. But what about friendships that lead you *away* from Christ? Can that happen?

As Christians, it's easy to want to be a good influence. We feel as if we have something really great (eternal life, for starters), and we want to share it with other people, especially the people we care about. That's a good thing. We talked about how we weren't put here to "hide our light under a bushel basket". We were meant to shine our light up on a hill, where people can see it. We're supposed to be examples of good Christians and to lead people to Christ. To do that, we can't associate *only* with other Christians. We need to venture out among the pagans sometimes, right?

True. Just as Jesus partied with tax collectors, we shouldn't shut people out simply because they don't believe what we believe. Everyone is created in God's image and likeness and is loved by Him. We need to do the same—to reflect His love to everyone we meet. That doesn't mean "I'm going to pretend to be your friend because then I can tell you about God." It means being a *real* friend to those around us and being a good example.

Sometimes, just by doing that, we can have a real influence on someone's life. I'm sure that, as a result of knowing you, some people around you have reevaluated their lives. I'm sure some have turned away from sin. Some may know Christ better, or pray more, because of you.

But sometimes it can work the other way. Sometimes friends, especially boyfriends or girlfriends, can lead us *away* from Christ while we're trying to lead them *toward* Christ. That's bad.

It's usually not a blatant thing. You're not scared. You know you're a strong Christian, and you know you're not going to stop *believing* in Christ. This person can't affect your faith—no one could ever convince you He doesn't exist or that He doesn't love you. So you're safe.

But ask yourself this: How does this relationship affect the *practice* of your faith? Have you made this person the center of your life, instead of God? Do you pray less regularly because of this relationship? Do you "deny Christ" around this person or this person's friends, in order to gain acceptance?

Most important, does this relationship cause you to sin? There are a lot of different ways a friendship or relationship can lead you into sin. Does this person gossip maliciously and draw you into it? Does this group abuse drugs or alcohol? Do they destroy people's property?

When Dating Leads to Sin

One of the most common, and serious, ways that a relationship can lead us away from Christ occurs when a dating relationship leads to sexual sin. When you're attracted to someone, it's natural to want to bring him closer to Christ. But when you're *sexually* attracted to someone who doesn't share your standards for sexual purity, you've entered a *very* dangerous situation. When the hormones get flowing, logic tends to go out the window. If you're with someone who doesn't believe in saving sex for marriage, or who doesn't at least *fully* respect your commitment to it, you're with someone who has no reason not to want to go farther. And when your resistance is down, you will be pretty likely to follow.

A *lot* of Christians get into this situation. Sexual sin happens in a relationship over and over, and they find it very difficult or even impossible to stop it. Either one person just isn't as committed to chastity as the other is or habits are just too ingrained, or whatever. But the person rationalizes staying in the relationship, saying

"But because of me, he's closer to Christ. He even goes to Mass once in a while."

But at what price? Repeated mortal sin is putting your soul in danger, as well as the soul of the person you're with. That's not the way to lead *anyone* to Christ. It's pretty much a guarantee that your relationship *won't* be infused with the grace of Christ. It's a guarantee that you're going to struggle, both emotionally *and* spiritually. It will be an impediment to the other person finding Christ, and it will keep you away from Him in the process.

If you're in a relationship that's leading you to serious sin, it's important that you realize that the sin *has to stop*. No ifs, ands, or buts. You're risking your immortal soul as well as the other person's. Eternity is resting on this. The stakes could not possibly be higher. You have to look at what's going on and take *serious* action to stop it. That means, if it's sexual sin, never being alone together, or staying out of the house/car/wherever there's a problem/ etc. You need strict rules, and you need to follow them. Get help if you need it.

A lot of people in this situation think, "I'll just keep going to confession every time it happens, and I'll be fine." Wrong. Think about it. *Repenting* means saying to God, "I'm sorry this happened, and I'm going to try really hard to make sure it never happens again." That's what it means to be sorry. That's the condition of your forgiveness. You need to be committed to changing things.

Just going back to the same old habits isn't going to cut it. If you do that, you know perfectly well it's going to happen again. You can't just say, "I'll go back into that tempting situation/being in a dark room alone/

making out in the car/whatever. Only this time I'll be stronger." No, you won't. Your hormones aren't made that way. And going into a situation where you're pretty sure you're going to sin is a sin in itself. That's right. You can sin before you've even started sinning, just by going back into a situation where you've repeatedly lost control, if you have no reason to believe you won't again except "I'll try really hard." Confessing means committing to make serious changes, committing to avoid those situations.

If that doesn't work, you need to end the relationship. Period. I know that may sound harsh, but think about it. Who is the god of your life? God? If so, what's worth jeopardizing your relationship with Him? What (or who) could be so important that you would risk losing Him? Where would you be without Him?

John Paul II says that it's God who "opens our hearts to friendship". If a friendship is ruled by real, unselfish love and true concern for the other, He will be there. Sin is a lack of that love, and if a friendship is marred by persistent, serious sin, real love is not in action. You can say "I love you" all day, but you're not loving, and God is *not* there.

God is love. He is the Author of love, and if we want real love in our lives, our relationships need to reflect Him, His standards, and His love. Without Him, relationships don't work, and love doesn't work.

29

Talk to My *Parents?*

Parents and older people sometimes feel that they have lost contact with you, and they are upset. . . . Sometimes you are very critical of the world of adults, and sometimes they are very critical of you. This is not something new, and it is not always without a basis in life. . . . I am asking you to build bridges of dialogue and communication with your parents.

— *John Paul II, Manila, 1995*

It's not always easy to have parents, especially when you're a teenager.

Basically, the problem boils down to this: you see yourself as a totally self-sufficient, independent entity who doesn't really need *anything* from them, except perhaps meals and health insurance and unlimited use of their car and bail money when you get into trouble. They, on the other hand, see you as a five-year-old with a driver's license.

There's bound to be trouble. You're gradually becoming more independent, and you think you can do it all, and they see you stepping out into a world they've seen a lot of, a world you may not be *quite* mature enough to handle. You want to let go, they want to hold on.

The truth, of course, is somewhere in the middle. You really *do* need them—probably more than you realize, but less than they think. But no one is ever very good at finding that happy medium.

The good news is, this is nothing new. The Holy Father even points this out. Every era has had some kind of tension between generations. They criticize you; you criticize them. And he says that these criticisms are sometimes justified. Neither teenagers nor adults are perfect, and each is really good at spotting the flaws in the other.

But beyond all of this lies the most important fact: they love you. Even in this world of broken families and rampant dysfunction, a vast majority of parents love their children more than anything and want more than anything what is best for them. And most teenagers love their parents—even though they may not want to admit it.

In a world where not nearly enough people love you, wouldn't it be nice actually to get along with the ones who love you the most? Not just "do whatever they say without asking questions", but really *like* them the way you used to, enjoy being around them once in a while, and work *with* them instead of *against* them?

This is what the Holy Father is talking about. He didn't say, "Just shut up and listen to your parents." Instead he asked you to "build bridges of communication". That's different, and it's both a lot easier and a lot harder.

Communication is a two-way street. It doesn't mean that they lecture you, and you just sit there and nod. Neither does it mean that you tell them off and get your own way. It means each understanding where the other is coming from and working toward a common ground.

Communication doesn't start with telling your parents where *you're* coming from or how you feel. It starts with finding out how they feel. "But I already know how they feel. They won't let me do what I want to do. They want to lock me up. They worry too much." But ask yourself this: What exactly are they worried about? Why do they make those rules that seem way too strict for you? And then, after you've asked yourself, ask *them*. Not rudely, not confrontationally, but nicely. Just tell them that you want to understand what their concerns are so that together you can work out solutions you're both comfortable with.

Once they've regained consciousness and recovered from the shock of your new cooperative attitude, it's time to pick them up off the floor and get to work. As they give you their reasons (or attempt to give you their reasons—it may not be easy), really listen to what they're saying. Ask questions—not to argue, but to get to the deeper reasons. Try to understand. Put yourself in their shoes for a few minutes.

Believe it or not, they were teenagers once upon a time. They went to parties. They even dated once or twice.

Try to look objectively at what they're saying, instead of just reacting defensively. If they say they don't want you to date yet because they're afraid you're not strong enough to say "no" and that you could be manipulated, think about it. Are you *really* strong enough to look someone you're absolutely crazy about right in the eye and say "No, I won't do that" even if it means losing that person? If you're not sure, then your parents may have a point.

Once you've heard everything they have to say, it's time to help them understand how *you* feel, and to address some of their concerns directly. If they don't like you dating someone because they're worried you may have sex, I'm sure it would be a huge relief to hear from you that you've decided to save sex for marriage (a good decision to make—see chapter 9) and about the steps you've taken to ensure that. Once they've heard that, they may be willing to soften their stand a little bit. And together you may be able to work out some even *better* ways of ensuring it. Believe it or not, they were teenagers once upon a time. They went to parties. They even dated once or twice. And it probably wasn't a whole lot different from what it is for you. They really do understand at least a little of what you're going through. But they're at the other end of it, and they have a different perspective. Try at least to find out what that perspective is.

Of course, none of this means you won't still have disagreements. It's part of the gradual, liberating, painful process of becoming an adult. But if you really make an effort to listen to them, to understand them, and to help them to understand you, you can make life a whole lot easier for everyone. It's amazing what a little communication and some active, careful listening can do to smooth the transition.

Epilogue

It really bugs me that formal religious education in America generally ends with confirmation. For the life of me I can't figure out why anyone would want to send people out into an adult world with an eighth-grade understanding of their faith.

John Paul II has messages that challenge you to go beyond a limited understanding of "religion". He wants Christ—the living, active Christ—to be an ongoing, active presence in your life. He wants you to understand Christ in an adult way and to develop an all-encompassing relationship with Him. He wants your faith to be more than just something to "do" on Sundays. He wants you to have an abundant life that you won't find with an immature, lukewarm faith.

I hope this book has helped you to understand a little better what John Paul II is saying to you about Christ and your faith. But this is the end of the book. Don't let it be the end of your faith life. Start working to live the life to which you've been called. Make time for prayer every day. Receive the sacraments regularly. Become a part of the life of the Church. Keep learning about your faith. Read John Paul II's messages in their entirety, especially the messages to youth. You can find them at any Catholic bookstore.

Remember that John Paul II loves you, and I love you. More important yet, Christ loves you, and He's waiting for you to come to Him, so that He can fill you up and give you that abundant life He promised when He was here.

Don't keep Him waiting.

For Further Reading

On Christian Life

Kreeft, Peter. *Your Questions, God's Answers*. San Francisco: Ignatius Press, 1994.

Lewis, C. S. *The Great Divorce*. New York: Macmillan, 1981.

————. *The Screwtape Letters*. New York: Macmillan, 1981.

Sheen, Fulton. *Treasure in Clay*. San Francisco: Ignatius Press, 1993. This is particularly good for those interested in the priesthood.

On Sexuality

Groeschel, Benedict. *The Courage to Be Chaste*. New York: Paulist Press, 1985.

Harvey, John. *The Homosexual Person*. San Francisco: Ignatius Press, 1987.

Hillerstrom, Roger. *Intimate Deception*. Portland, Ore.: Multnomah Press, 1989.

Trobisch, Walter. *I Loved a Girl*. San Francisco: HarperCollins, 1989.

On the Catholic Church

Catechism of the Catholic Church.

Keating, Karl. *What Catholics Really Believe*. San Francisco: Ignatius Press, 1995.

On Prayer

Guardini, Romano. *The Art of Praying*. Manchester, N.H.: Sophia Institute Press, 1985.

———. *Meditations before Mass*. Manchester, N.H.: Sophia Institute Press, 1993.

On Abortion

Nathanson, Bernard. *The Abortion Papers*. New York: Frederick Fell Publishers, 1983.

Wilke, Jack. *Abortion Questions and Answers*. Cincinnati: Hayes, 1991.

Acknowledgments

Thanks to Pattie Philibosian, for her much-needed organizational and editorial assistance.

Thanks to Michael Flach and Ann Marie Pacia of the *Arlington Catholic Herald*, for originally publishing the columns which became the basis for this book.

Thanks to Kelly, Siobhan, Pattie, Rox, and Jack, for their unflagging support for this and all of my other projects, and for being the best friends on the face of the earth.

Thanks to the staff of Ignatius Press, for all of their hard work in converting my manuscript into a book, and for remaining my friends through it all.

And a special thanks to Joseph Fessio, S.J., not only for publishing my book, but also for creating the educational and employment opportunities which have made such a difference in my life and have made my work possible.